All you need to know about talent

development in sport

Kristoffer Henriksen, Carsten Hvid Larsen
& Louise Kamuk Storm

All you need to know about talent development in sport

ATHLETE INSIGHT PRESS

All you need to know about talent development in sport
By Kristoffer Henriksen, Carsten Hvid Larsen & Louise Kamuk Storm

© 2024 Kristoffer Henriksen, Carsten Hvid Larsen, Louise Kamuk Storm & ATHLETE INSIGHT PRESS

First edition, 2024

ISBN 978-87-975109-0-2

Photos: page 18: Keld Lund for Viborg Elite; pages 32, 56, 66, 150, 172, 226: Büro Jantzen for Team Denmark; page 46: Andreas Bastiansen for Svendborg Talent & Elite; page 80, 196: Team Danmark; page 90, 130: Jan Christensen for Dansk Håndbold forbund; page 108, 142, 186: private photos; page 120, 214: Jacob Vinholdt for Talent Billund; page 160: Viborg Katedralskole; page 204: Ole Mortensen for Holstebro Elitesport; page 236: Fagfotografen v. Geir Hauksson for Svendborg Talent & Elite. Thank you for allowing us to use your photos in our book.

The book was originally published in Danish by Content Publishing. Thanks to Birgitte Lie Suhr-Jessen for editing the Danish version.

To all you talent developers.

*Every day, you're dedicated to creating great development environments.
You're passionate about developing young people who are passionate
about developing themselves.
It's important work.*

*Together, you show the world how far diligence and care can help young
people reach.*

*For decades, coaches, managers and talent developers have engaged with
our research, asked us questions and challenged us. Thank you for that.*

*It is in the meeting between science and practice that we can make a
difference together.*

Meet the authors

Carsten, Louise and Kristoffer are among the world's leading experts in athletic talent development. As researchers in the Psychology of Sport, Excellence and Health research group at the Department of Sports and Biomechanics at the University of Southern Denmark, they have conducted extensive research on the challenges of talent development, including training, specialization, talent development environments, coach roles, mental health, and more. Together and individually, they have authored numerous books on the subject and published over a hundred scientific articles in reputable international journals. Additionally, they possess substantial insights into talent development in practice through their applied sport psychology work in Danish and international talent development and elite sports.

Content

Foreword: Bold communication of rigorous research   11

Chapter 1: A sustainable philosophy   19

Part 1: Mentally strong and healthy young athletes   31

Chapter 2:   Develop drive   33

Chapter 3:   Promote a holistic skills package   47

Chapter 4:   Open up to obstacles   57

Chapter 5:   Handle mental health   67

Chapter 6:   Foster mental fortitude   81

Part 2 Sustainable talent pathways   93

Chapter 7:   Foster many, cut few   95

Chapter 8:   Allow for ample avenues to the world elite   109

Chapter 9:   Tolerate talent transfer   121

Chapter 10:   Facilitate fruitful feedback   131

Part 3 Holistic talent development environments   **141**

Chapter 11:   Cultivate caring connections   143

Chapter 12:   Reward responsible role models   151

Chapter 13:   Embrace the entire environment   161

Chapter 14:   Promote parental partnerships   173

Part 4 Sound talent cultures   **185**

Chapter 15:   Grasp group dynamics   187

Chapter 16:   Assist athlete autonomy   197

Chapter 17:   Encourage knowledge exchange   205

Chapter 18:   Cultivate culture   215

Part 5 Dynamic sport organisations   **225**

Chapter 19:   Stimulate stakeholder synergy   227

Chapter 20:   Explore your environment   237

Mind your mission moving forward   247

About the authors   251

Bold communication of rigorous research

One day, we were enjoying our lunch together. A good colleague was visibly frustrated and we asked why. He had just had an unfortunate experience. The day before, a journalist had contacted him about a topic in which he is an expert. The issue was complex, and he had explained all the nuances thoroughly and in detail. Now he had received an email from the journalist. She had chosen not to use his quotes. It had been too specific, she said. Instead, she had chosen to quote an 'expert' who had nowhere near the same expertise. This expert, on the other hand, had left out the complexities and was sharp and precise.

This led to a good discussion about research and communication. The colleague's experience brought an important issue to the forefront. Researchers are experts in their fields. But researchers often write and communicate in inaccessible language in inaccessible scientific journals. As a result, society turns to other experts who do not have the same precise knowledge, but have the courage to be clear.

Personally, we have always been committed to communicating our research directly to users. We have always seen it as one of the university's core tasks to disseminate knowledge. It is no use sitting on the couch and fretting about how many self-appointed experts in talent development and sports psychology give voice to half-baked conclusions based on outdated data on a daily basis. We need to step up to the plate.

While we were enjoying our lunch and talking to our good colleague, a young and highly ambitious coach in another part of town not far away had just been hired for his dream position as a talent development manager. In his eagerness to prepare himself well, he started searching for research in the field.

He quickly became discouraged. He found a lot of material, but found it hard to distinguish substantiated knowledge from loose, experience-based opinions. The research articles were hidden behind a paywall. He picked up the phone and called his former university lecturers, the authors of this book. We helped him along, but agreed that it is all too easy to get lost in the search for knowledge.

These two experiences gave us the idea for this book. We decided to write a book based on thorough research, both our own and that of international researchers. We have searched the scientific databases and we have contacted our international colleagues. It is in our DNA. Scientists are often cautious. The world is complex and knowledge is rarely definitive. However, we also decided to muster the courage to throw caution to the wind. We decided to write a book that presents clear strategies and precise recommendations. That is also in our DNA.

Courage combined with solid scientific grounding.

The result is this book.

Danish design

The thinking that forms the basis of this book has grown out of its context, Denmark. Denmark is a small country and has always had to produce deliver world-class talent development against the odds. Our strategies have had to compensate for a small population, a limited geography and insufficient budgets. It has forced us to punch above our weight. It has forced us to bring out the best in every ambitious young athlete. It has forced us to create inclusive development environments. It has forced us to forge strong ties between research and practice. By making a virtue of necessity, our challenges have become our greatest strengths.

In Denmark, we have always strived to share knowledge, which we also do with this book. But it is not without a slight tremor. Imagine if one day the great nations succeed in creating development environments as good as we see in Scandinavia.

Talent development is hot

Talent development is a hot topic these days. The debate on how to best support the highly talented and motivated has now become legitimate on par with the debate on how to safeguard the weakest.

In sports, there has long been a focus on talent, but never before have so many resources been invested in talent development as right now. In professional sports, especially football, talent development has become big business, as the ability to develop your own talent has become the main source of revenue for clubs. But even in smaller sports, good talent development is a prerequisite for successful elite ventures.

In culture, certain industries have a long tradition of systematic talent development, such as the Royal Danish Ballet, but also in many other branches of culture, the focus on talent development has grown. In Denmark, there are local talent schools in music, film, performing arts, etc.

The Danish school system has also seen an increasing focus on talent development. A number of exciting initiatives aimed at stimulating talented young people in the natural sciences, social sciences and crafts speak volumes.

In the business world, too, there has long been a focus on talent, especially in terms of developing leaders and specialists. Although talent development of adults in a career perspective is far removed from the young sports talents, we find that talent managers in large companies are inspired by sport.

Our expertise comes from sport. We stick to it.

We do not want to come off as experts in areas we do not have real research-based knowledge about. On the other hand, we have no doubt that the knowledge we present in the book can also inspire talent development outside of sport.

Talent development is tricky waters

Denmark is not the only place where modern society is described as a performance society, where young people are constantly having to perform and where they are either losers or winners. It is exciting and stimulating, but also difficult. Too many talented young people struggle with stress and unhappiness.

We know there are many dilemmas in talent development. How to balance results and long-term development, people and medals, resilience and well-being, sporting and personal development, autonomy and control, knowledge sharing and trade secrets? The dilemmas are plentiful.

Good talent development is about much more than heart rate zones, kicking techniques and nutrition. There is a need for concrete humanistic strategies for talent development. We need to develop strategies that ensure talented young people can fulfil their potential without jeopardising their well-being and mental health. Young people deserve this.

That is the point of the book.

You are the target group

The book is aimed at talent development practitioners. If you are a talent coordinator or manager in a club or at a school, this book is for you. If you are a talent manager in a federation or municipality, this book is for you. If you are a coach in youth sports, talent sports or elite sports, this book is for you. If you are a parent of a child who is interested in sports, this book is for you.

If you work with talent development in the arts, in the school system or in business, you need to start translating the book's messages to your field of work. We are sure you will find ideas, arguments and knowledge to inspire your practice.

If you are a student in higher education or a coaching programme, we hope you are reading this book because a forward-thinking teacher has put it on the curriculum. This book is definitely for you too.

Book structure

The book is divided into five parts, focusing on concrete strategies and practices. Our ambition is to translate good and healthy values and attitudes into sustainable actions. A philosophy only comes to life when it is put into practice.

In the first chapter, we present a talent development philosophy. A solid research-based and value-driven philosophy that puts the environment at the centre and has its heart in the right place.

Part 1, Mentally strong and healthy young athletes, puts the athlete at the centre. It is about motivation, life skills, mental strength, and how to use adversity and take responsibility for the well-being of your talented athletes.

Part 2, Sustainable talent pathways, focuses on the pathways to the world's elite. Based on themes such as talent identification, specialisation and talent transfer, we offer suggestions on how you can organise training that really works.

Part 3, Holistic talent development environments, puts the talent environment at the centre and directs your attention to meaningful relationships, role models, education and parents.

Part 4, Sound talent cultures, focuses on psychological safety, warmth, care and respect. How to build culture on good, healthy values, with your heart in the right place.

Part 5, Dynamic sport organisations, looks at the talent organisation itself, at effective interactions and at the importance of continuously exploring, evaluating and developing your own organisation.

Our vision is for sport to lead the way in cracking the code to one of modern society's biggest challenges. To show that environments can support achievement and well-being at the same time. To teach young people to be ambitious without being (too) self-critical, goal-oriented without losing touch with the present moment, and dedicated without losing the joy. That a good life does not stand in the way of good results.

Enjoy your reading.

CHAPTER 1

A sustainable philosophy: Environment-centred and guided by the heart

Well-founded, well-functioning talent development is based on consistency between what people say and what they do. Consistency in what different actors in the talent community do.

All talent developers work from a set of basic assumptions and values about what produces development. When these basic assumptions are reflected, clarified and coherent, we can talk about a philosophy. A coaching philosophy or a talent development philosophy. Unfortunately, not everyone working in talent development is aware of their philosophy, has thought about it or written it down.

An intentional talent philosophy creates consistency. When you as a talent developer are consistent in what you do, you avoid uncertainty among your colleagues and athletes about what you stand for and what your long-term goals are. Certainty creates focus.

When you as a talent developer are aware of your philosophy, it becomes easier to be clear. To make choices in difficult situations, justify your choices and decisions, and stick to your decisions. To build trust and gain support from the talent, their parents, coaches and other relevant stakeholders.

Philosophy as a concept sounds very abstract, but a philosophy is of great importance in daily practice. As a coach, manager and talent developer, you are constantly challenged. Perhaps your talent philosophy includes thinking long-term and encouraging young people to train on their own to develop autonomy. But suddenly an opportunity to win a youth championship arises. It just requires you to push the youngsters and manage their training with a firm hand. It is easy to get caught up.

Good and consistent talent development in practice is only possible when it is based on a clear philosophy that is not deviated from. Even if there is a possibility of short-term results rather than long-term development. Solutions to the many daily challenges only become coherent when they are based on clear values and beliefs.

In this chapter, we offer a clear philosophy built on a solid and research-based foundation. We offer a standpoint from which you can create sustainable talent development in our society. What we mean by *sustainable is* summarised in a mantra at the end of this chapter.

While there are many ways to go, not all practices are created equal. A philosophy should be backed by solid and recognised research.

What is a talent philosophy?

A talent philosophy is the talent developer's foundation. It is a description of the values and core beliefs you want to guide your actions and provide answers in difficult situations.

It is more than a 'what doesn't kill you makes you stronger' statement and less than a textbook with all the key research findings.

No one lives up to all their values in all situations, 24 hours a day, 365 days a year. That does not change the fact that a clear set of values will make it easier for you to follow your values and act as the leader and talent developer you want to be.

When we use the term 'talent developer', we think of anyone who is tasked with helping young people develop.

The philosophy

Here are five core ideas that can form the foundation of a long-lasting research-based talent philosophy.

Mission: People come before podiums!

Struggling to reach your potential must be meaningful when you play sport. Otherwise, you will not develop. It should never just be about medals, results and turning 'meat into gold'. Many young talents never experience winning gold in international competitions. Regardless, young people deserve to feel that their hard work is meaningful when they put a lot of time and effort into it.

Talents are people first – sports talents second. The goal of talent development is not just to create great athletes, but well-rounded, whole young people. The goal is for young talent to acquire the skills and competencies they need in their pursuit of excellence, not just in sport but also in life. You should always aim for young people to develop as:

- *Motivated participants.* That children and young people learn to love their sport for a lifelong perspective and develop a motivation that extends beyond adolescence. It's about participation and attachment.

- *Master of life.* That young people do not just become good at their sport, but acquire skills and resources that can benefit them in other arenas and at other times in life. It's about personal development and quality of life.

- *Medal winners.* That those who want to are given the opportunity to become as good as they possibly can. You cannot predict who will end up as medal winners, so everyone should have the right to quality training. It's about equal opportunities and performance.

Young talents deserve that you, as a talent developer, want to develop them towards something that goes beyond their medals. But what? One thing could be to learn how to deal with adversity.

Adversity is natural and inevitable in both sport and life. You cannot avoid losing and failing. When a young talent is trying out a difficult new skill, doubt and worry will be more frequent guests than confidence and joy.

Young people are not made of glass. You do not have to prevent athletes from facing adversity. Adversity has the potential to build young people's courage and mental strength. Adversity can teach athletes to treat themselves and their teammates with care and respect when they make small mistakes, when they miss deadlines or when they experience stagnation.

But young people are not made of stone either. They can only take so much and there is no need to cultivate adversity. We know from a century-long research tradition in developmental psychology that children and young people develop strong self-esteem if they are met with empathy and unconditional love, and if they learn that they have value irrespective of their achievements.

You must have the courage not to clear the path for the young athletes and free them from adversity. However, adversity in itself does not make you strong. Sport should teach young people to handle adversity with care and acceptance. This will benefit them in many situations throughout their lives.

Another way that you as a talent developer can help young talents look beyond medals is developing their ability to be fully present in what they do. When you 'help' children and young people plan and ensure an 'optimal everyday life', you forget their true strength; the ability to be fully present and immersed in their sport. Focus is the currency of development. We will always prefer athletes who can be fully present in their training, but are a bit disorganised in their training plans, rather than athletes who have written down dream goals and sub-goals and know exactly how many minutes before a training session they should eat, but plan and evaluate in their mind while training.

And then there is *compassion*. It saddens us to see how many young people adopt a very self-critical and perfectionist approach to their sport. When they experience adversity and defeat, they dive into a toolbox that contains only one tool, the big hammer to hit themselves in the head with. They evaluate themselves harshly in the quest to show the world that they are ambitious. In the pursuit of becoming even better. But it is too hard to always be so self-critical. We believe that young talents who learn to meet themselves with care, with compassion, will be able to build a motivation that is based more on love for the sport and less on the fear of having to pick up the hammer again.

In other words, good talent development environments have the potential to develop young people not only as athletes but also as people. We believe that as a talent developer, you can be proud if you manage to teach young people:

- To work not only on their sporting, but also their personal development

- To be aware of their values as athletes and human beings

- To experience meaningfulness, for example by being role models and giving back to the community

- To treat themselves, their teammates and their opponents with respect, even in times of adversity and defeat

- To lose a game without losing heart

- To join a community and ask for help

- To demonstrate autonomy and take responsibility for key elements of their career.

Motives: Young athletes are not miniature grown-ups

We are all familiar with the images of national team athletes winning world championships. In the daily training environments, there are many stories of incredibly hard training sessions and anecdotes about large training volumes. These stories are inspiring, also for the coaches who will be running the club's youth training later in the day. No one becomes an expert in any field without years of intense dedication and training, but that does not mean that you as a youth coach have to accelerate the development of the young athletes.

Children and young people are not miniature adults. They cannot deal with the same exposure or develop in the same way as adults. Throughout puberty, periods of stagnation are replaced by quantum leaps in both physical and cognitive development. So under no circumstances should a talent developer or youth coach copy the programmes of established elite athletes.

A key task for the talent developer is to understand their target group and adapt the training to their physical and mental capacity.

When talent developers rush things, allow kids to specialise early and primarily put them in targeted, coach-led, adult-like training, they typically create athletes who perform well in adolescence, but unfortunately, not always as senior athletes. They drop out due to stress, injuries, lack of well-being or loss of motivation.

Allow young talents to participate in other sports, do a variety of workouts, play games, and on their own initiative train with friends. They will develop a broader foundation of motor skills and psychological attributes, find it easier to switch sports, if necessary, acquire a stronger base of intrinsic motivation, and achieve a much more complete personal development. They will acquire social skills from being part of different communities and an ability to adapt to changing demands, which they will need as senior athletes.

In the same spirit, sports should strive for competition formats that match the developmental stages of young people and support their long-term development. Today, we often see sports with a competitive structure that promotes winning at an early age, which is in direct contradiction to sustainable long-term talent development. Competition formats should be designed to take into account development differences among children, stimulate skill development rather than early physical development, and to not demotivate young children or youth who are late-developers compared to their age group.

The goal of talent development is to create athletes at the highest international senior level. Youth results should never be the goal of talent development, and a good youth or talent development coach should never be measured by the number of youth champions they have coached. A talent developer should be measured by the ability to work long-term to develop talent that will later become world-class senior athletes. The purpose of competing as a youth athlete is not to win, but to learn how to compete.

Milieu: Personal growth is nurtured in good sport environments

A strong and cohesive environment is a prerequisite for strong individuals, just as a healthy environment is a prerequisite for individuals with a healthy approach to their sport.

Some environments are far better than others at nurturing and developing elite athletes. It is not just what happens on the training field that is important in understanding why some athletes develop into elite athletes while others do not. The whole environment is key.

Overall, we know that a good talent environment is characterised by a coherent structure. Young people face many conflicting demands. Their school teachers think that school is the most important foundation for a good life. Their coach thinks that sport is very important. Their friends think there should be room for fun and a night out. And their parents – well, it can be hard to know what they think. A good and coherent structure in a talent development environment means that all players talk to each other and create synergy. This is a prerequisite for creating athletes who thrive, develop and ultimately stay in the sport.

Meaningful relationships either open up development opportunities or create strong values for the individual. Meaningful relationships are built on empathy, trust and mutual respect. This means that in a relationship, people can openly and honestly share their joys and frustrations without fear of being rejected or weeded out.

Empathy is crucial. Being able to put yourself in someone else's shoes and understand the world from perspectives other than your own is important for building meaningful relationships. Talents use meaningful relationships when they need advice, when they have doubts and when they face adversity. There is a great responsibility in both engaging in such relationships and in creating the environments that provide the framework for meaningful relationships.

In a small country like Denmark with few athletes and big ambitions, it makes perfect sense to shift the focus from talented athletes to talented development environments. And this makes just as much sense for other countries with a desire for socially responsible talent development.

Mental health: Thriving is a result of sustainable cultures

Culture is everywhere. It is all the unwritten values and rules. It is just the way *we do things around here*. Successful environments have strong cultures with alignment between appearance and action, between what you say you do and what you actually do. This creates clear expectations and peace of mind to focus on the task at hand. Cultures need to be strong because the characteristics of the culture become the character of the athletes. A culture of knowledge sharing among coaches and management develops athletes who are good at sharing knowledge and being inspired. As a talent developer, you can create any number of strategies – if they do not fit the culture, they will never work. Fortunately, culture can also be managed and developed.

Not all cultures are equally good. An essential element of successful cultures is psychological safety. This means that everyone can contribute ideas and ask questions without fear of being laughed at or belittled. You are being heard. In cultures with a high level of psychological safety, all ideas and skills are brought into play and young people do not spend their energy on self-preservation and saving face. They spend it learning and developing.

You often hear that elite sport is demanding and tough. That coldness and cynicism are inevitable at the top. We do not agree with that. And even less so when it comes to talent development. We believe in warmth and caring for one another, and that it is not only possible, but optimal, to build successful talent development environments on care and respect. Having your heart in the right place.

Mental health is not only an individual matter. Elite and talent development environments can build or break down the mental health of young people. We have seen examples of cultures being allowed to develop where athletes' mental health has been put aside in the pursuit of medals. No number of medals can justify such practices. But we also see environments that have a clear positive impact on young people's mental health. In our view, athlete well-being should be included as a metric when an environment evaluates its success.

We believe that in this challenge lies a whole new justification for talent and elite sport. We have long known that talent development and elite sport should be about more than medals. We used to say that young people in sport learn determination and dedication. Today, many young people struggle with stress. They have probably become too good at determination and dedication. Today's society is a performance society, and young people experience performance pressure in many arenas. Imagine if sport could take the lead in developing ways for young people to perform and thrive at the same time. For them to be ambitious with the one life they are given without compromising their mental health. That has to be the ambition.

Might: With great power comes great responsibility

As a talent developer, you have a lot of power and influence in the lives of young people. With that power comes great responsibility. It requires humility. It should stimulate you to continuously stay up to date and curiously seek knowledge.

Knowledge about talent development is expanding all the time. Talent development is big business. Research is being conducted into many aspects of talent development, and our knowledge is becoming more precise, nuanced and contextualised. That is why research, education and development are cornerstones of good talent development. We believe in the value of coach education, of systematically evaluating your own practice, of participating in research projects and of peer coaching.

With expert roles comes power and influence, and managing this power requires a high level of legitimacy. Perhaps you have had the experience of giving a quick piece of advice to a young person in passing? As a talent developer with a lot of power and influence, you need to think carefully about what you say to talents. They are listening.

The responsibility does not just lie with the individual talent developer. In dynamic talent environments, people work closely together. You discuss philosophies and values, are curious about each other's practices, give each other feedback, develop. You work as a team. You coordinate with each other so that young people experience coherence and wholeness. The school system is flexible when young people have to go to training camps, just as the sport supports young people going to school camps. You look at the bigger picture – not just the sport, but the young person's entire life.

MANTRA

We can summarise it with a simple mantra:

TALENT DEVELOPMENT IS

FOR AS MANY PEOPLE AS POSSIBLE,

FOR AS LONG AS POSSIBLE,

OF THE HIGHEST POSSIBLE QUALITY

AND WITH THE HIGHEST POSSIBLE DEGREE OF MEANINGFULNESS

Talent development environments should be inclusive. Both because a large community motivates and because you cannot predict with any real certainty who will end up being good.

Talent development environments need to be designed to keep athletes motivated and stay with them as long as possible. Both because it takes a long time to get good and because the goal is to create senior elite athletes.

Talent development environments must strive for the highest possible quality. Both because a focus primarily on training volume increases the risk of injury and burnout, and because a focus on quality in training and socialising is crucial for development and well-being.

Talent development environments must consist of processes that are experienced as meaningful by the athletes, also outside the narrow realm of sports. Both because many end up not becoming world champions and because the purpose of sport is also to create educated young people who generally experience meaning and value in their lives.

This is what we mean by *sustainable* talent development.

Part 1

Mentally strong and healthy young athletes

In the book's foundation, the talent philosophy, in chapter 1, we started by proclaiming that young talents are people first and potential medal winners second. That the goal of talent development is not only to create great performers, but well-rounded, whole young people. We argued that as a talent developer, you need to relate to the young people's drive, understand their sense of what is meaningful and support not only their sporting, but also their personal development.

In this first part, we focus on the individual talented athlete, or rather the individual young person. We will present research-based knowledge and provide concrete recommendations on how you can work with motivation, initiate mental strength and life skills training, use adversity constructively and take responsibility for the talent's mental health and well-being.

Remember, a philosophy only comes to life when it is put into practice.

CHAPTER 2

Develop drive

The vast majority of young people in talent sports are highly motivated. They may have many different motivations, but they have a strong fire burning inside them, a driving force beyond the ordinary. Unfortunately, it is easy to organise training in such a way that this fire slowly burns out. So they lose sight of their motivation and the meaning of it all. We recommend that you develop an environment where the drive can thrive and develop.

On the outskirts of a medium-sized town, we find Thomas. He is getting ready to coach the club's U14 team. Thomas has arrived in good time. He is picking up cones, vests and balls for the day's training. He believes that good preparation and a well-thought-out training programme are important for the players' long-term development. Thomas is not a real-life person, yet he can be found in many clubs around the world. Thomas is both no one and everyone. Thomas is an amalgamation of many coaches we have met.

Thomas is not new to coaching. It has been just over seven years since he first started coaching his son's team. It started as it often does, with his son's team needing a coach. Thomas has always had a coach at heart. He has not talked about it much, but since he was injured as a player, he has always wanted to be a coach. He occasionally dreams of making a living out of it, but for now it is a hobby alongside his job as a middle manager at a company in the city.

When Thomas started coaching, he was hooked on the technical and tactical aspects of coaching. He read, found drills and watched a lot of matches. In his eyes, the ideal coach was a smart coach with an understanding of the game. However, Thomas quickly realised that this was not the key, either to coaching children or young talent. He discovered that his ability to create motivational training was more important than his tactical understanding. The players went home happy after having fun, playing a lot and enjoying themselves. They did not show the same level of enthusiasm when he introduced a smart system of play. However, Thomas' understanding of motivation has changed, partly as he has become more experienced and partly because he has completed a number of coaching programmes where he has developed greater insight and had the opportunity to discuss with other coaches.

When he first started out coaching, he was more outgoing and used a lot of competition in the game. Training became very intense and there were many small battles in training. Without realising it, he mainly rewarded the players who won the duels, were tough and ran a lot. This was reflected in many drills. They practiced penalty kicks, and those who scored got to kick again. The others had to stand and watch. The losers had to clean up after practice. For matches, Thomas picked the team he believed could win. It was often the same players. Sometimes he would bring players to games without them getting any playing time. During the match, Thomas would often shout loudly, especially when the team was behind, to instil fighting spirit and energy in the players. If the team won, Thomas would buy the team sodas.

Thomas realised that his intention was not to create an environment that was inappropriate for learning and development. He wanted to create an environment that nurtured the players' drive. Where the focus was on friendship before rivalry. A healthy development environment for young footballers. Thomas knew that motivation is a prerequisite for learning. He had just become too focused on winning. Let's get back to what Thomas learned in a moment, but first you need to understand some key concepts.

What are the key concepts?

Motivation has often been defined as a process that adds intensity and direction to a particular behaviour. Motivation is linked to a multitude of factors, including an athlete's basic motives, basic needs, the belief that they can succeed and social support. More precisely, we define motivation as 'the direction and intensity of the athlete's efforts that arise from the interplay between the athlete and his or her motives, experiences and needs on the one hand, and the athlete's environment, including the coach's style, specific training exercises and the culture's core values on the other.'

Dropout describes when an athlete quits their sport.

What do we know?

Every day, young talents go to practice. They are often – but not always – motivated to go. Often, they go because they just love their sport. Sometimes because they have made a commitment to the team and the coach. Other times because they know that is how they can achieve their goals. And sometimes, they need a nudge from their parents. But once practice is underway, most athletes often find it both fun and meaningful. At best, there are moments when they forget about themselves and everything around them and are just deeply engaged in the activity.

Motivation is a core concept in sport. In youth sport, researchers have used the concept to investigate why children start playing sport, why some stay and others drop out, why some become good and others do not, why some choose one sport and others another. We are particularly interested in the link between motivation and learning, the importance of drive in the acquisition of skills. High-quality learning requires drive, mental energy. Drive is key to remembering and using what you have learned. What you learn with high engagement is more nuanced, better remembered and more easily applied.

Talent development is a learning process.

Motivation is based on basic needs

Back in the 1970s, motivation research centred on intrinsic and extrinsic motives. Workplaces were concerned with how to use extrinsic factors such as reward systems, evaluations and bonus schemes to increase effort and productivity. But there was also an emerging understanding that intrinsic motivation might be more genuine and enduring. In the mid-1980s, Edward Deci and Richard Ryan, two renowned American psychologists, wrote their first book on what they called *self-determination theory,* which would later become one of the dominant motivational theories in sport and exercise.

Today, self-determination theory is a complex matter and provides a broad framework for the study of human motivation. It is multi-layered, including a view of basic human psychological needs and a description of different levels of intrinsic and extrinsic motivation. One of the strengths of the theory is that it does away with the simplistic idea that people are either driven by intrinsic or extrinsic motivation and that these are opposites. In fact, motivation is constantly shifting. An athlete may well be extrinsically driven on the way to training because he knows he will be scolded if he stays away, but during training he slips into being fully engaged in the activity for the sake of the activity. At the same time, Deci and Ryan introduced many more forms of motivation on a continuum from intrinsic to extrinsic. One of these is *identified regulation,* which means that an external reward is internalized and attributed personal importance. For example, a handball player may be motivated to do strength training, but this motivation could be the result of coaches and others telling her that strength training is necessary for her to achieve her goals.

In our view, however, the most central part of self-determination theory is that it accurately identifies three basic psychological needs that are inherent and that we humans strive to fulfil. In other words, they drive our motivation:

1. The need for autonomy covers a need to take initiative and have influence. *I am in charge of something.*

2. The need for competence is the need to feel that you as a human being have mastered something, are learning and developing. *I can do something.*

3. The need for relatedness is a need to engage in meaningful, close and long-term relationships with other people. *I belong with someone.*

Let us return for a moment to Thomas, a youth coach who had just been introduced to self-determination theory in a coaching programme. At home, one evening after a long day of training, he wondered to what extent his training met these three needs. Not enough, he quickly realised. He always had a specific plan and managed the training with authority. It was effective, but it got in the way of the players' need for autonomy. They were never part of decision-making. He did not ask for their assessment of a training session, but always told them what they had done well and not so well. In terms of competence, it looked better, he believed. The league table reflected this. Still, he was not sure that they each experienced competence in training, especially when he pointed out mistakes, which he did regularly. Creating relatedness was harder, he realised. They were a team, no doubt about that. But obviously, they were also rivals. He had encouraged them to compete against each other to create a competitive spirit and intensity. The best got the most playing time. He had also sometimes separated good friends because their levels were too different.

Thomas made a decision. He wanted to create a motivating youth environment based on the three needs. He started small. He started involving the players in decisions, gave them small tasks, let them do the warm-up. He evaluated with them rather than evaluating them. He asked what they were keen to learn and helped them identify when during training they could practice it. He emphasised individual learning and development over team results. He made an effort to build community, ensuring that everyone felt important, that everyone got playing time, that everyone played an important role on and off the field. He organised fun activities outside of practice.

Thomas understood the subtle message of the theory. Motivation varies. As a coach, you cannot always create situations where athletes experience true intrinsic motivation. But that does not mean you have to reward or punish to create extrinsic motivation. As a coach, Thomas had to strive to stimulate players to adopt and identify with extrinsic motives, to want what they have to do. So he told them about the importance of certain exercises and training methods. Making them understand so that they felt that the motivation to train came from within.

It took time, but Thomas saw how the players changed. The mood was different. The motivation was different. The players seemed more willing to mobilise the mental energy it takes to learn something.

Not everyone is motivated by winning

Goal orientation theory is a recognised motivational theory that deals with motivation in a performance context. It starts with the need for competence, the idea that the most motivating thing for any athlete is to experience improvement. But how do athletes measure their improvement?

A *performance-oriented* athlete experiences competence when she is better than others around her. She constantly compares herself to others. She cheers when she wins. A *mastery-oriented* athlete experiences competence when she masters a new skill. She is oriented towards mastering her tasks. She cheers when she succeeds with an inswinging corner kick for the first time, even if others can do the same.

Athletes who are only performance-oriented do not push themselves to their limits when they are already the best in a group. They prefer exercises where they can confirm that they are the best, rather than new and difficult exercises. When they move from a small to a larger club or from junior to senior and are suddenly not among the best, the core of their motivation will be threatened.

Athletes who are only mastery-oriented focus solely on the process. They are more concerned with developing than being the best. Therefore, they are good at dealing with adversity.

The two ways of being motivated are not either-or. In practice, it is an advantage when athletes are driven by both performance and mastery orientation. They grit their teeth in competitive situations and are motivated by being better than others. But in times of performance adversity, they are good at staying focused on the process and finding motivation in developing their skills one step at a time.

As a coach, you influence athletes' motivation through the 'motivational climate' you create.

In a *performance climate,* the focus is on competition. Who is the best and who is the worst? This happens when you motivate using competitive elements and praise those who win. When you take a special interest in the athlete's performance goals. In a *mastery climate,* the focus is on mastery, learning and process. It arises when you highlight and acknowledge effort and development, create collaboration and encourage athletes to improve. When you are primarily interested in the athlete's process goals.

This was also new to Thomas, who had always created a performance climate. It had provided a good intensity, but he could recognise the problems. Especially how the players preferred exercises they were good at and were a bit reluctant when they had to learn new exercises where they risked appearing worse than the others.

Environments motivate

Motivation does not just reside in the individual. It is not just psychological fuel. The environment has a decisive influence on the extent to which young talent engages in training and competition. In other words, the environment can support the innate drive or work against, disrupt and diminish it.

We have been at the forefront of recent research into talent development, which has shifted the focus from the individual athlete to the good development environment. The central question in this research has been what characterises good talent development environments that manage to develop many senior athletes. We return to this research several times throughout the book.

Although this is not a theory of motivation, the results have spoken for themselves. Some environments are far more successful at supporting athletes' motivation, well-being and development than others. Good talent environments may be different, but they also have common traits. Here we have selected three of the characteristics of good development environments related to motivation:

1. Firstly, these positive environments have ambitions to develop autonomous and socially competent athletes, not just to develop athletes' technical and tactical skills. They fulfil the athletes' need to develop competence.

2. Secondly, there is room for free initiative. You can train in the facilities on your own and outside of normal practice hours. Athletes are encouraged to take initiatives to develop and influence training. In other words, there are good opportunities to fulfil the need for autonomy.

3. Thirdly, the environments are characterised by supportive training groups. There is a focus on community. The group is composed of young talents and experienced athletes of different skill levels. Everyone has a role in the group and everyone is expected to learn from each other and from themselves. So they have an eye for relatedness.

In other words, good development environments are designed to address the basic psychological needs of athletes, so that athletes are motivated. The point here is that motivation does not reside in the individual, nor in the environment. Motivation resides in the encounter between the individual and the environment.

This was what Thomas had come to realise. It did not make sense to be annoyed when players lost focus and engagement during his practice. He had to take responsibility for creating a motivating environment. For Thomas, it became a point of no return. He understood his coaching role in a new way. He further realised that the theory did not just apply to the players, but also to himself. He took several courses to develop his competence, he sought out coaching colleagues to feel related, and he searched for his own coaching philosophy to experience autonomy. He participated in building a learning environment for the club's coaches. All of this motivated himself and his players.

Motivating environments reduce dropout rates

The most important prerequisite for young talented athletes to become successful senior athletes is that they do not drop out along the way and thus do not make it to the senior level at all.

Research has identified many reasons why young people drop out of sport. They fall into five main categories: lack of enjoyment in training, lack of a sense of accomplishment, social pressure and high expectations, physical challenges such as injuries, and conflicting priorities. It is not uncommon for high expectations in both school and sport to coincide with identity development, with young people starting dating while trying to figure out who they are.

Young talents are generally extremely motivated. They really want it. But it is not hard to kill their inner fire. Endless repetition without variation. Constant evaluation based only on results without focusing on the learning process, followed by a period where the results do not materialise. Being separated from your best friends. Becoming a master at sitting in the backseat because you have to play at another club far away.

Of course, it is only fair that some young people want to do something else because there are so many other exciting things going on in their teenage years. But it is a shame when the dropout rate is due to talent environments killing motivation, when the environments do not meet the athletes' basic needs for autonomy, relatedness and competence. When the coach becomes so controlling that autonomy disappears. When internal competition to create intensity comes at the expense of a sense of belonging. When there is so much focus on correcting mistakes that athletes never feel good enough. A survey of Danes' sports habits shows that a poor environment is the cause of 27 per cent of all dropouts among 13-15-year-olds. We are convinced that the same is true in other countries.

What can you do?

Great talent developers understand that motivation is not something athletes are born with or without, have or do not have. They understand that motivation does not reside in the individual, is not a personality trait. Instead, motivation arises in the encounter between a specific athlete and the environment created by the talent developer.

We do not like the idea that the coach has to motivate anyone. After all, it is really the talent that has to put in the effort to learn. But athletes' motivation is shaped by how you organise practice, how you set up goals, how you evaluate, how you involve athletes in decisions, how you stimulate community and much more. As a talent developer, you can stage the environment in such a way that young people want to put in the effort to learn.

Great talent developers recognise that motivation varies over time. There are periods where other things naturally take precedence. When a young talent starts high school, it is only natural that for a period of time, their energy is directed towards making friends, testing themselves in dating, delving into school topics and much more. Skilled talent developers find room for this.

As a talent developer, you should first and foremost recognise the huge role you play in developing motivation and take that responsibility upon yourself.

What do we recommend?

- Take an interest in why your athletes started playing sports. What do they love about the sport? What is their drive?

- Create an environment that allows athletes to fulfil the three basic psychological needs: autonomy, competence and relatedness.

- Do not stifle athletes with rigid tactical plans, one-sided training and high performance expectations. Instead, let them develop as people who need to gain experience, test themselves, and who, at times, are preoccupied with other major challenges in life than sport.

- Create a mastery climate where you focus more on learning than results. Set process goals with individual athletes and the team and make sure you evaluate the process goals.

Literature

Larsen, C.H. & Alfermann, D. (2017). Understanding dropout in the athlete development process. In: J. Baker, S. Cobley, J. Schorer & N. Wattie (Eds.) The Routledge Handbook of Talent Identification and Development in Sport. London: Routledge.

Ryan, R.M. & Deci, E.L. (2017) Self-Determination Theory – Basic Psychological Needs in Motivation, Development, and Wellness. The Guilford Press.

Roberts, G. C., & Nerstad, C. G. (2020). Motivation: Achievement Goal Theory in Sport and Physical Activity. In The Routledge International Encyclopedia of Sport and Exercise Psychology (pp. 322-341). Routledge.

CHAPTER 3

Promote a holistic skills package

We recommend that you, as a talent developer, take responsibility for developing the life skills of young athletes. Life as a young talent is demanding. It requires skills both on and off the field. Young people with life skills are more likely to succeed both on field and later in life. But life skills are just that. Skills. And skills need to be trained and developed.

In 2018, Daniel Gould visited Denmark. He is one of the most influential researchers in the field of sports psychology and co-author of the world's most widely used book for teaching the subject at universities around the world. Daniel is also one of the researchers who has worked extensively with the concept of life skills.

He was on his way to Halmstad in Sweden to be a reviewer for a PhD thesis, and we asked him if he would swing by Copenhagen and Team Denmark, the official Danish elite sport institution. We wanted him to give a presentation to Danish youth coaches on the topic of sports psychology for young athletes and life skills.

We knew Daniel from a meeting the year before during a conference in Seville. Daniel was smiling and accommodating, but we had talked about how that meeting probably made a bigger impression on us than him. Did he know who we were?

Already at the airport, our worries were put to rest. He greeted us warmly and asked about one of our latest articles he had recently read. He referred to the meeting in Seville.

On the taxi ride from the airport to Team Denmark, we talked about what he was doing at the moment. His work as a professor at Michigan State University was not as extensive anymore because he was approaching retirement. But some people cannot fully retire, and Daniel had several research projects going on. And now here he was, on his way to give a talk. Daniel was humble. Instead of highlighting his own research, he talked about the books he was currently reading. One of the books was about Generation Z and how young people today see their phone as an extension of their arm. They do not hold the phone. They *are* it. That is why it is not so easy to just tell them to put it away, even though coaches and educators sometimes find that it gets in the way of learning. It would be like asking them to cut off their hand, he laughs. "We need to understand young people on their terms," he says, sounding nothing like a professor approaching retirement. "But that is not the same as giving up," he emphasises, "because we have to want something with them."

What are the key concepts?

There are several concepts that are related to life skills in different ways.

Positive youth development, PYD, is fundamentally about promoting positive youth development through sport and other venues. Researchers have shown how to engage young people in their communities, such as schools and sports clubs, in a way that is productive and constructive. By recognising and working with young people's strengths, providing opportunities and fostering positive relationships, sport can be used to create positive development. In other words, it is not about becoming good at sport, but about using sport to develop as a person.

Life skills describe psychological skills, attitudes and dispositions acquired or modified through education or experience that are used to deal with adversity and challenges that arise in daily life, in and out of sport.

In the US, researchers have focused on life skills as skills acquired in sport that benefit young people in other arenas. In Europe we have focused on life skills as skills that can be acquired anywhere, but are essential for young people to handle life as a talented athlete – both in and out of the sports arena.

What do we know?

On the road to elite performance, young athletes will inevitably face adversity and challenges. There are periods of extra pressure, such as tough training periods or periods where competitions and exams overlap. Young people also face many transitions that require them to adapt to new circumstances or demands, whether in sport, school, social life with friends or family. Many of these transitions often happen at the same time. Classic examples include the transition to a better club, a senior team, moving away from home, moving from elementary school to high school, etc. The consequences for athletes who cannot adapt to these challenges and demands are often a drop-out from the sport

Life skills can be many skills

What are the skills that influence whether young talent can handle the transitions, busy periods and life as an athlete? Well, they can be quite a few. We could mention goals, motivation, planning, collaboration, communication and many more.

Fundamentally, life skills are basic abilities that are crucial to a person's development and well-being. Is the young person good at cooperating with others in the training community and asking for help, or does she come to believe that she has to do everything herself? Does the young person have some sense of the meaning and structure of the overall training plan, or do all training sessions and seasons seem equally crucial? Can the young person make autonomous decisions? Can the young person plan their daily routine and find time to recharge, or does everyday life become unnecessarily stressful with bad habits around sleep, homework and eating?

Life skills are not skills you necessarily see directly on the field and in training or competition. But you see them anyway. Do your athletes show up calm, energised and focused, or do they breeze in at the last minute eating a chocolate bar while pre-occupied on Instagram? It affects the quality of their training.

Some life skills are more important than others at different points in your career

As sports psychology consultants, we have experienced coaches and parents contacting us for help because children aged 10-12 lacked a competitive, winning mentality. In our eyes, this was the wrong focus. With a solid grounding in research, we have for years emphasised that children and young people need a broad and holistic package of psychological skills to manage their careers.

For pre-pubescent children, the talent developer's most important task is to create a mastery environment that focuses on individual learning and development rather than results. You can do this by starting to introduce concrete process goals in training. You can help talents evaluate the process, not just the outcome, and both what went well and what did not. And you can introduce short visualisations of specific elements of exercises that they struggle with. We call it learning skills, and the work never stops.

Later, during puberty, young people are ready to work on their social skills. Athletes who are unable to engage constructively in a training group, for example because they are unwilling to compromise, do not share knowledge with teammates or only see others as competitors, end up struggling. So it makes sense to focus on the ability to collaborate, encourage each other, seek help and share knowledge. That work never stops either.

Around the time athletes finish elementary school and start high school, they find that school demands more of their time. They have more homework, the school day gets longer and social media takes up more space. The same is happening in sports. The number of training sessions per week increases and they become more demanding. It is also during this time that many athletes start experiencing adversity for the first time, such as sitting being benched, changing clubs, not being at the same level as the best, minor injuries, etc. During this period, it is crucial that young people are able to create a life that focuses on sport, but also leaves room for a good life outside of it. It is also about being good at making important choices, focusing on high-quality training, dealing with adversity and planning your everyday life so everything all fits together. Having the courage to prioritise. It is especially important for athletes to develop these skills during this period, but again, this work never ends either.

One thing at a time. Our belief is that once athletes have mastered these basic skills needed to learn and train with quality and make life work, it makes sense to focus on performance skills.

Life skills can be trained in many ways

During Daniel Gould's aforementioned lecture at Team Denmark on sports psychology and life skills for young people, an ambitious young coach states that he can see all the points. He agrees that some athletes are not good enough at managing everyday life. And that it has to come first. "But what should I do in practice?" he asks. "How do you train life skills?"

Gould smiles, fully aware of the complexity. He looks like someone who has faced this question many times before. He starts by emphasising that life skills do not come out of nowhere. They must be trained, developed and given attention in everyday life. In addition, he distinguishes between two approaches.

Working *explicitly* with life skills means that life skills are practiced and talked about in the environment. For example, a swimming club may work systematically to prepare swimmers to deal with everyday life. This means that coaches or other experts talk about why they are important, specifically help swimmers to get an overview of everyday life, and follow up and evaluate this. In this way, life skills become something that is practiced like any other skill.

Working *implicitly* with life skills means that life skills are rarely talked about and only practiced indirectly. This does not have to be a bad thing. Daniel gives an example of a coach who often asks athletes before training what they remember from the last training session and what they would like to focus on in this one. In another example, after a training session, the coach often asked the athletes if there was anything they were unsure about. When they brought up a challenge, she did not just answer. Instead, she would ask the athlete who in the club might be able to help and encourage the athlete to ask them. In this way, the athletes developed the skills to set goals and ask for help, but without ever being told it was something they had to learn.

"But which method is best," asks the aforementioned trainer. "They are not mutually exclusive," Daniel replies with a smile. "On the contrary. They complement each other very well."

What can you do?

Sport can be a great place to develop important life skills. But it does not always happen. When coaches or parents send the wrong signals, when environments encourage unhealthy internal competition, or when coaches micromanage and control athletes, athletes do not develop autonomy and life skills. It is important to ensure that sport fosters the positive development of young people. That sport creates opportunities for them to learn valuable life skills and develop positive values through sport.

Daniel Gould is very concerned that what young people learn in sport benefits them in other areas of life, such as school or work. He calls it 'transfer'. Transferring knowledge. During his talk at Team Denmark, Gould gave examples of several coaches who were good at creating transfer. For example, he told of a wrestling coach who taught her athletes how to transfer skills between domains. She talked to the athletes about what they learned in sport and how they could use those skills in school. She also indirectly acted as a role model by talking about how her method of doing group feedback rounds was actually something she had first encountered in her civilian job. She showed that, like all people, she learns many different things in many different contexts and that creativity is about pushing boundaries.

What do we recommend?

- Work consciously with life skills. Life skills do not just happen. They need to be developed through training and practice throughout the environment, in the weight room, at school and in training. You can do this in many ways. Implicitly by developing a culture that emphasizes a healthy view of competition versus only winning, showing interest, asking questions and providing small challenges. Explicitly by holding workshops, helping athletes get an overview of their schedules and much more. And preferably both.

- Work from a clear leadership philosophy with a focus on development. You must dare to prioritise personal growth. Initiate activities and exercises that create reflection, accountability, curiosity and stimulate athletes to ask for help. In your leadership philosophy, success should be understood as personal growth and development.

- Build positive relationships among athletes. Good, deep, long-term and reciprocal relationships create a sense of belonging. As a talent developer, make sure you dedicate time for athletes to get to know each other and form strong relationships on and off the field.

Literature

Collins, K., Gould, D., Lauer, L. & Chung, Y. (2009). Coaching Life Skills through Football: Philosophical Beliefs of Outstanding High School Football Coaches. International Journal of Coaching Science, 3, 29-54.

Gould, D. & Carson, S. (2008). Life skills development through sport: Current status and future directions. International Review of Sport and Exercise Psychology, 1, 58-78. DOI: 10.1080/17509840701834573.

Holt, N.L., Neely, K.C., Slater, L.G., Camiré, M., Côté, J., Fraser-Thomas, J., MacDonald, D., Strachan, L. & Tamminen, K.A. (2017). A grounded theory of positive youth development through sport based on results from a qualitative meta-study. International Review of Sport and Exercise Psychology, 10:1, 1-49. DOI: 10.1080/1750984X.2016.1180704.

Ronkainen, N., Allen-Collinson, J., Aggerholm, K. & Ryba, T. (2022). Beyond life-skills: talented athletes, existential learning and (Un)learning the life of an athlete. Qualitative Research in Sport, Exercise and Health, 1-15. DOI: 10.1080/2159676X.2022.2037694.

Turnnidge, J., Côté, J. & Hancock, D.J. (2014). Positive Youth Development From Sport to Life: Explicit or Implicit Transfer? Quest, 66:2, 203-217. DOI: 10.1080/00336297.2013.867275

CHAPTER 4

Open up to obstacles

Adversity is inevitable in talent development.

Young athletes are not made of glass. They can withstand adversity. They can even learn from it. Through adversity, they can develop mental strength, but more importantly, they can learn to treat themselves and their teammates with care and respect in the face of adversity.

But young athletes are not made of stone either. They can only take so much. There is no reason to cultivate adversity. Children and young people who are met with support and empathy, and who learn that they have value regardless of their achievements, gain a strong sense of self-worth.

We recommend that you acknowledge the bumps in the road that athletes face and actively use them to create resiliency. You should not clear the path for them, but note that adversity in itself does not make them strong. Young people need to learn how to deal with adversity. It will benefit them in many situations throughout their lives.

Meet Rob Book. He has just completed a PhD thesis on talent development in severely disadvantaged and tough areas in the US.

Rob is from Canada. Before coming to the University of Southern Denmark to write a PhD, he worked as a teacher and coach at a US school. The school was located in a troubled area. Every year, the school counted how many students were still alive. Too many had lost their lives to drugs and shootings. The school was located in an area characterised by gang activity, low income, crime, ethnic challenges and a general lack of hope. Rob saw how some kids managed to use sport as a way out, while too many wasted a huge talent. They never found their place in the sport, despite wanting to and having the potential. He wondered why some of these troubled talent environments succeed in helping young people move on, while others just let talent slip through their fingers.

Rob interviewed athletes who had succeeded against all odds. He interviewed coaches and managers, both in the severely disadvantaged talent environments and in the clubs that the athletes later ended up in. And he followed a specific basketball environment over a period of time. Rob found that traditional talent environments failed to accommodate these athletes. The athletes were talented, but did not fit into the environments. They did not have good support and backing from home. They were not used to structure, making schedules and setting goals. They lived from day to day. They were used to drawing strength from being members of a strong group, a gang. Too often they succumbed when they took to the streets with their opportunities for community and quick money. On the other hand, the environments in which athletes succeeded in their sporting careers despite the circumstances were unique. Here, coaches went far beyond the normal coaching role. The environments offered an attractive community that was strong enough to keep the young people off the streets. There was at least as much focus on teaching athletes how to deal with life as there was on teaching them sporting skills.

During his PhD, Rob started reading about adversity. He read articles that argued that adversity is necessary for development. He read that all the best athletes could point to periods of adversity and that these periods had strengthened them. He even read a research article titled 'Talent needs trauma'. He felt researchers were celebrating adversity and going too far.

Rob thought back to his own time as a coach in the troubled Atlanta neighbourhood. He thought about how often he saw crime, shootings and violence. He thought about young people who had to be part of a gang to survive because, for example, dad was in jail and mom was working three different jobs just to make ends meet. As a coach, Rob had had to spend thousands of dollars out of his own pocket on food, transportation and equipment for the athletes, and he had to provide massive personal support to them. He thought that this kind of adversity had not been beneficial to the athletes. On the contrary, he found that adversity was a tough opponent and that his basketball players needed support to make it.

Rob realised that the debate about adversity needs to be nuanced. A player with good support from home in a healthy training environment can learn a lot from facing adversity in the form of losing, being benched, playing against someone bigger, failing an exam or missing a flight. Especially if they get help to deal with it and see it as a learning opportunity. Athletes without solid support, on the other hand, do not benefit from more adversity, especially in the form of a depressing events, losing a parent or an anxiety-provoking attack. Athletes may need bumps in the road, but they do not need trauma. In this respect, athletes are no different than any other human being.

What are the key concepts?

Adversity describes a situation or circumstance that is difficult or associated with difficulties over a short or long period of time.

Bumps in the road is partly synonymous with adversity, but is often used for shorter and more concrete challenges, such as losing a spot on a team, being benched, losing a try-out, etc.

Resilience refers to a person's ability to cope when life is difficult and come back stronger after difficult periods of threat, crisis or stress. Resilience is often described as three processes, i.e.: (a) the ability to identify protective resources; (b) the ability to access these resources when needed; and (c) the ability and motivation to return and use what was learned. Resilience is not about being invulnerable and able to withstand anything, but about the ability to bounce back from difficult experiences in a positive way.

What do we know?

Research shows that resilience is not a trait that athletes do or do not have. It is a trait that can be developed. Resilience is only developed when you face adversity and use that adversity constructively to learn about yourself, your resources and the resources in your environment so you can come back with new insights.

Adversity can be empowering

So, adversity is necessary to develop resilience. In talent development, we sometimes see a tendency to clear the path for the greatest talents. But you can clear it too much. We sometimes see that the best youth athletes have almost never lost, never been dropped, never been benched. We see that their parents are so supportive that the young people have never forgotten their lunch or shoes. Unfortunately, we also see that when these athletes encounter the harsh realities of the senior ranks, there is a good chance they will quit. They simply have not developed the ability to deal with adversity. Sheltered athletes rarely make it all the way because they do not learn to navigate 'rough waters'.

"A smooth sea never made a skilful sailor," Franklin D. Roosevelt wrote many years ago. If a sailor only ever sails when the water is calm and flat, when the sun is shining and life is harmonious, there really is no need for great skill. It does not take much when things are going well. Conversely, if a sailor seeks out training on days when the wind is blowing and the waves are pushing the boat, the sailor learns to look out, make decisions and handle the boat.

Training in light winds is a prerequisite for handling medium winds, and training in medium winds is a prerequisite for handling high winds. This is how you learn to handle life's storms step by step.

Adversity can break you

But the wind can be too strong, the adversity too harsh. Let us go back to Rob Book for a moment. His clear conclusion was that the athletes he interviewed had succeeded in the face of adversity. Not because of it. The adversity they experienced had been harsh, and all of the athletes could point to others who were just as talented, but did not make the cut. They gave up, ended up in gangs and, disturbingly, often as victims of a shooting.

Rob interviewed coaches and managers in the professional environments that later welcomed the athletes from difficult backgrounds who succeeded. They unanimously shared that athletes carry their upbringing with them like 'invisible tattoos' and something that always gets in their way.

In other words, adversity is not always good. It can be too much, and not just in the US. We have also experienced difficult issues in our work with world-class athletes. We have met athletes who struggled in practice, whose parents were going through a divorce and at the same time experienced a death in the immediate family, which of course impacted their mental health. With help, the athletes overcame the challenges. From this vantage point on the other side of the challenges, they said that on the one hand, it had been educational and that a major crisis made it easier to deal with smaller crises later on. But they also said that they had been very close to giving up the sport and that they would not wish something like this for anyone else. And most importantly, they said that if they had not had the right help, they would not have looked back on the crisis as a learning opportunity. This brings us to the final point.

Adversity cannot stand alone

The athletes in Rob's research who came through despite adversity all had coaches who saw sport as an arena for personal development; a place where athletes could become more balanced people with better well-being and more resources. They had coaches who prioritised their personal development and schooling before their athletic skills. They had coaches who saw their vulnerability behind the tough exterior and helped them as people.

In 2019, Christopher Bryan and his colleagues wrote a review article on resilience in sport and business. We will not cover all their points here, but we will note that adversity does not create resilience in itself. Bryan first described how adversity is necessary. If athletes do not experience adversity, they will keep doing what they are doing. They do not develop.

But that is not enough. Bryan went on to describe how after major or moderate challenges or adversity, athletes will experience a decline in resilience. They become drained of resources. This period is crucial for there to be a point later on where the athlete thinks differently. Bryan describes this as a metacognitive process. Athletes learn about how they deal with adversity, what resources they have and how to best activate them. This allows them to come back a more resilient version, ready to face new challenges. In physical training, we talk about supercompensation. Hard training first creates physical exhaustion and then, if you recover, increased strength. If you train too hard too often, your training will be wasted because your body does not have time to compensate. It will not come back stronger. The same goes for the mind.

Adversity requires a period of reflection and learning afterwards. And here, athletes often need support in the process.

What can you do?

Overall, there are three points here. First, there is no need to clear the path for athletes. Adversity is empowering. Second, there is no need to create unnecessary adversity in the pursuit of resilient athletes. There is plenty of adversity in everyday life. Third, you need to make an effort for athletes to learn from the adversity they face. It does not happen by itself.

Let's take an example. A young football player naturally experiences adversity in everyday life. He faces players who are better. He goes through a difficult transition from one year group to the next. He experiences periods when training demands clash with assignments and exams. He gets a new coach. He gets benched. He is late and gets scolded. He sees good friends drop football. He experiences periods of pain and does not know whether to fight through it or be careful not to get injured. He is faced with difficult choices, including offers from other clubs and choosing between an important match and a school trip. He gets a girlfriend, loses a girlfriend, gets a new girlfriend. He gets into a fight with his mom or dad who thinks he is doing too little or too much. He loses a family member to illness or sees his beloved dog get run over.

All of this is perfectly natural. But it is also quite a lot to deal with. Your goal as a talent developer is to make sure the player learns from the natural adversity. Do not create extra adversity. You make sure he learns from adversity by talking to him: "What did you experience? What did it do to you? How did you move on? What inner resources were you able to draw on and what strategies worked? Who could you lean on?" And then your job is to point ahead when the player faces new adversity, for example, when moving to a new club or a new level: "What did you learn the last time you went through something difficult? How can you apply it now?"

What do we recommend?

- Allow adversity. Do not remove obstacles in front of the young athletes. It is not your job to send out text messages with reminders before practice, pack their lunches and do their laundry. Take responsibility for ensuring that the fundamentals are in order, for example that there is a dialogue between club and school, but do not smooth out the rough edges. Have an ongoing dialogue about what healthy types of adversity athletes should experience in your environment.

- Do not create artificial adversity. You do not need to tell the bus to leave early so an athlete is left behind. And if you want three young kids to lose to a couple of older and stronger athletes, make sure they learn from it.

- Help process adversity. When athletes experience periods of adversity, either in sport or outside of it, create space for 'supercompensation'. You should ensure that there is time to recharge and that athletes are stimulated to reflect so they actually come back stronger.

- Draw parallels to the next adversity scenario. Remember to occasionally talk to athletes about what adversity scenarios are coming up. Help them see that what they have learned from previous adversity can be applied again.

Literature

Book, R., Henriksen, K., Stambulova, N. & Storm, L.K. (2021). "All they have seen is a model for failure: Stakeholder's perspectives on athletic talent development in American underserved communities". Journal of Applied Sport Psychology. DOI: https://doi.org/10.1080/10413200.2021.1958953.

Book, R., Henriksen, K., Stambulova, N. & Mathorne, O.W. (2023) "We are their last chance": A case study of a college basketball environment in an American underserved community, Journal of Applied Sport Psychology, DOI: 10.1080/10413200.2023.2183281

Book, R., Stambulova, N. & Henriksen, K. (2020). Oatmeal is better than no meal: the career pathways of African American male professional athletes from underserved communities in the United States. International Journal of Sport & Exercise Psychology, 19(4). DOI: 10.1080/1612197X.2020.1735258.

Bryan, C., O'Shea, D. & MacIntyre, T. (2019). Stressing the relevance of resilience: a systematic review of resilience across the domains of sport and work. International Review of Sport and Exercise Psychology, 12:1, 70-111. DOI:10.1080/1750984X.2017.1381140.

Henriksen, K. (2018). Dare to Prepare for Reality: Helping National Orienteering Team Athletes Handle Adversity. Case Studies in Sport and Exercise Psychology, 2(1), 30-35. DOI: 10.1123/cssep.2017-0016.

CHAPTER 5

Handle mental health

Top athletes master the ability to have high ambitions, bite the bullet and do the impossible. Young talents on their way to the top sometimes do it even more. This requires athletes' networks to focus on their well-being, wellness and mental health.

We recommend that talent developers consider athlete well-being as a measure of how well their talent environment is working, in line with athlete development and performance. You should aim to create a healthy environment where athletes achieve their sporting goals, but do so in a way that still allows them to thrive, have fun, be whole people and not experience undue stress. Mentally healthy athletes in a healthy environment.

Mental health is on everyone's lips, and for good reason. Sport is about more than medals. Very few talented young swimmers, sailors, runners, badminton players and rowers end up on the podium at the Olympics or world championships. Only very few young boys and girls who chase dreams and balls around the field end up as professional football players. That's why you should strive for more with your deed in sport than creating that one world champion. We described in chapter 1 that the purpose of youth sport should rightly be to develop *motivated participants*, *masters of life* and razor-sharp *medal winners*. Motivated and mentally healthy athletes simply win more medals, especially in the long run.

Both in Denmark and around the world, we have recently seen scandals about mental health – or rather the lack of it. Athletes have come forward and spoken out about unhappiness and harsh environments. There have been clear examples of cultures being allowed to develop where athletes' mental health has been put aside in the pursuit of medals. This is not compatible with a modern sporting system that values the person behind the athlete.

In our quest to understand mental health in elite sports, we reached out to one of the researchers who knows the most about mental health in elite sports, Andreas Küttel. Andreas is currently a researcher at the University of Southern Denmark, but he has a long and impressive career as a professional ski jumper for Switzerland. Andreas has participated in three Olympic Games, has won several World Cups and in 2009 became world champion in the large hill event. He knows the nature of the sport. Ski jumping is a sport where you have to push yourself to the limit every day, and preferably a little beyond. Andreas has felt the anxiety on his own body. He knows how to ask himself if he really dares to do the next jump. At the same time, for many years he was the youngest athlete on the Swiss national team. He had to fight extra hard for his place. He could learn from the older athletes, but he also had to prove himself every day in an environment where the others were bigger, stronger and had had more years to build up their courage.

It is Friday, a cold and white winter day when we catch Andreas at his house in a small town in the countryside. He has built a garden shed for his exercise equipment. He has just completed a hard cycling workout on his hometrainer and answers the Zoom call with red cheeks and a smile on his face. We get the idea that you can take the man out of the sport, but you cannot take the sport out of the man.

Andreas starts by talking enthusiastically about both his good experiences in the sport and periods of adversity and pressure. We feel that we hit the nail on the head when we contacted him to learn more about mental health in elite sports. Andreas is not just a good researcher. He has also experienced first-hand both when sport creates good mental health and when it challenges it.

What are the key concepts?

Let's first agree on what we are talking about before we get back to Andreas. Mental health, mental strength, well-being, wellness, etc. Although many people use these terms, there is actually no consensus on what they mean, let alone what they mean in a sports context.

According to the World Health Organization (WHO), **mental health** is a state in which people thrive because they can develop their abilities, cope with stress, engage in social communities and contribute to society. In other words, there are two dimensions. First, there is an experiential dimension, which is about feelings, specifically that people experience well-being and feel good about themselves. Second, there is a functional dimension, namely that they function in everyday life and under stress.

Well-being is defined differently in different contexts, but is usually about the experience of well-being, energy, drive and enjoyment of life. Note that well-being is, in a way, part of the definition of mental health. For the time being, we do not distinguish between the two.

Again, **mental ill-health** is defined differently, but is basically about not feeling good about yourself and others. It can vary in degree from a general tendency, to something that occurs for short periods of time, and from mild concern to actual clinical diagnosable disorders such as depression, anxiety and eating disorders.

Mental strength, or mental toughness, is something else entirely. It is about being able to stay focused and act according to plan when under pressure. Mental strength is therefore linked to performance. You can be unhappy even if you are mentally strong under pressure.

In this context, we use mental health and well-being as synonyms. The key thing you should take note of is:

- Mental health is more than the absence of mental illness and disorder. To have high mental health, it is not enough that athletes do not have depression or eating disorders. They need to feel like they can contribute, cope with the stresses of daily life and develop their abilities when interacting with others.

- The experience of mental health depends on the context. There are big differences between countries and sports. Experiences of stress and challenges that are problematic in one context may be acceptable in others.

- Mental health in sport needs to be based on the reality of sport. Generally speaking, it is important not to 'medicalise' the fact that young people experience pressure before exams and get upset when they lose a pet. It is neither stress nor depression, just healthy human reactions. Similarly, it is important to recognise the nature of sport. Feeling sad to get benched, having trouble sleeping before an important competition and worrying before the team for a big tournament is selected are not necessarily signs of poor mental health or unhappiness. That said, these experiences should not be frequent among young athletes.

What do we know?

Sport is good for mental health. The exercise, the community, the experience of contributing to a team, and the experience of becoming good at something. These are all factors that benefit mental health. We know this from research. This is also where Andreas Küttel starts his story. He particularly remembers when he was about 20 years old and got a young Swiss coach. The coach was interested in Andreas, not just as an athlete, but as a person. He asked questions. The coach was young and curious himself, and Andreas saw that the whole team together was discovering the recipe for world-class performance. It was exciting. Andreas enthusiastically leans forward as he emphasises how much motivation and well-being he experienced during that period.

Does this mean that athletes are immune to problems? Far from it. In fact, we would venture to say that there is reason to be vigilant. Why?

Ambitious athletes are often dedicated, perfectionist and self-critical. They have the ability to suck it up and keep fighting, even when they do not feel great. It is not always all good. At the same time, sport is often a harsh arena with focus on short-term goals and internal competition. Coaches and athletes push the boundaries. It is exciting and perhaps necessary, but not always without problems. Add to this the fact that athletes' everyday lives are characterised by tight schedules, time pressure, few holidays and training every day of the week. And if we look further, we see a so-called performance society, where young people experience being measured and weighed in many arenas.

All in all, you might be able to see that the stage is set for trouble. But what is the real story? Mental health is a relatively new research topic in sport and there is a lot we do not yet know. Nevertheless, we can highlight a number of key findings from research and practice.

We ask Andreas what is really important to know about mental health in sport. He is passionate about the well-being of athletes. He has a lot on his mind and is an avid talker.

Most athletes are doing well

Andreas Küttel has himself been involved in researching the well-being of Danish elite athletes, and he emphasises that the vast majority of Danish athletes are doing well. He emphasises that mental health is an important focus. But it should not only be about those who are struggling. There is a lot to be learned by understanding all the athletes who thrive and experience meaning. Who are they and what characterises their training environments?

Great athletes are not immune to mental health issues

While physical activity and the camaraderie of sport is good for mental health, and while many athletes are mentally strong under pressure, athletes are not superheroes. They are not immune to mental health challenges. Andreas' research in Danish sport shows that symptoms of anxiety, depression and unhappiness are found in all sports and across all age groups. It is not easy to compare athletes to the general population because researchers have used slightly different methods and slightly different age groupings. But internationally, there is a fairly broad consensus that the prevalence of mental health problems among talented and elite athletes is roughly equivalent to the prevalence in the same age groups in the general population. Women are more affected than men. Unfortunately, it is going the wrong way. Both among athletes and other young people, the prevalence of mental health challenges is on the rise.

Mental health and mental ill-health are linked, but...

This point is a bit difficult to understand, says Andreas. Research shows that mental health and mental ill-health are related, so athletes with high mental health usually do not have mental disorders. However, you can actually find athletes who score fairly high on well-being, but at the same time have a diagnosable mental disorder.

Perhaps one of the best examples is Michael Phelps, American top swimmer and one of the greatest Olympic athletes in history, who for much of his life has been happy with his training and daily life, but throughout his career has struggled with ADHD and at times depression.

How is this possible? First, it is important to understand that the origins of mental disorder are complex. Some people are more predisposed than others. So, depression does not have to come from a bad environment. Second, good daily well-being probably makes it easier to cope and live with a mental disorder. Sport offers a structured environment and community that, along with the physical activity itself, can act as medicine for mental health.

Phelps' story adds another layer to this understanding. When he stopped swimming, he got worse. His depression and ADHD symptoms took over. He missed the structure and community. He ended up making a comeback.

Mental health and peak performance are linked, but...

It would be an exaggeration to say that you can only perform when you are in balance and experience high well-being. There are far too many examples of the opposite, such as athletes winning medals in high-stress times and on a team experiencing conflicts. On the other hand, it is not sustainable in the long term. Being unhappy can only be sustained for so long.

In the long run, mental health is a significant resource. Athletes who experience high mental well-being generally stay in the sport longer. And that is a prerequisite for becoming *really* good. Athletes who do not thrive find themselves having to justify a hard life with good results. Suddenly, they are not just struggling to perform, but to make sense of a hard and meaningless everyday life. This rarely helps the ability to perform. In the long run, we can safely say that athletes experiencing high mental health win more medals.

Recharging is key

A few years ago, we participated in a research project. The goal was to understand stress and recovery during long-term competitions and training camps. The project was extensive and we followed four national teams during long journeys and continuously measured stress and recovery. In interviews, we asked about everyday life, training camps and competitions. Here are some of the key points:

- Many factors cause stress. It was clear that athletes have a stressful everyday life. Monotony, clique structures, high expectations, pressure to perform and finances were just some of the things that stressed them out. Sometimes it is a sum of many small things.

- Athletes who are good at recovery can handle a lot of stress. Often, the problem is not the athletes' batteries are drained by many different factors, but rather that the athletes are not good at recharging them. Andreas Küttel also remembers from his time as a professional ski jumper that it was difficult to balance the adrenaline rushes on the ski jump and relaxation. He used nature, but also relaxation audios several times a day for many years.

- Recovery is more than physical restitution. It is not enough to physically relax. Doing homework or planning workouts is not recharging. Some athletes could not actually tell us how they recharge. Those who could mentioned reading a good book and socialising, among other things.

Mental health is especially challenged at certain career points

A sports career is not a linear journey. There are major shifts along the way. Classic examples are the difficult transition from the junior to the senior levels and the transition in the school system from elementary to high school. And then there are all the small and unpredictable shifts, such as when an athlete gets injured. There are simply times when athletes are particularly vulnerable.

Even over the course of a season young people will experience varying levels of pressure. During periods of high internal competition before a try-out or during intensive training periods, well-being is harder to achieve. This is hard to avoid. But these periods should be short and followed by recovery.

Andreas Küttel has experienced the difficult periods first-hand. He talks about the time after the Vancouver Olympics in 2010, when everyday life got the better of him and he underperformed. He had just become a father. This meant that his lifestyle was uprooted. He was happy, but he was also worried because he did not prioritise his recovery and did not always get enough sleep. He had also had a conflict with his coach, which meant that they stopped working together. And he could sense that he was nearing the end of his career. He vividly describes how he sometimes thought: "No, this is not how I want to end it". During this period, Andreas was more vulnerable and did not have the energy he used to have. Fortunately, Andreas always had good people around him, which brings us to the last point.

Environments can support *and* threaten athletes' mental health

Some environments are more supportive of mental health than others. Mental health is strained when athletes face 50-hour 'work weeks', are shamed, bullied and taunted, or experience excessive and public weight control. No number of medals can justify such practices. But even more accepted practices can also create challenges, such as when young people are pushed to specialise too early and train uniformly at an early age, are pressured to train and compete despite injuries, and are not given time to recharge.

Fortunately, we find ourselves in many talent and elite environments where we see young people take responsibility and develop personally, where different adults talk about what is good for the young person, where there is focus on long-term development rather than short-term results, and where high ambitions go hand in hand with community. These are environments characterised by psychological safety, an appropriate overall load and clear values. When this is the case, sport can help strengthen young people's mental health.

Andreas Küttel says he would never have gotten through the tough times without a strong environment. In ski jumping, you have to face fear daily, and luckily Andreas' coach always asked him how he felt when he had experienced fear again. Andreas lived at home for a long time, so when he was home from his many travels, there was always a good base. Simon Ammann (four-time Olympic gold medallist) was his teammate for 15 years, but also his friend, and he was always in his corner. And for ten years, Andreas used his sports psychologist to put things into perspective.

Andreas has had different coaches throughout his career. On one end, the young, curious and engaging Swiss coach who always planned fun social activities when they were on a trip. He made them feel like a family. He involved the athletes in planning the strength training and Andreas was allowed to give small presentations on what he learned in his university studies. It was a time with a very flat hierarchy and lots of fun in daily training. At the other end of the spectrum, Andreas had a period with an authoritarian Eastern European coach who created a clear hierarchy and often expressed a lack of understanding that Andreas wanted to finish high school. Andreas vividly remembers their first meeting, when the coach stepped up to a podium and told him that from now on, this is how we do things. Andreas was only 16 years old and was OK being told clearly what to do, but he experienced it as a clash with Swiss culture, and before long he missed having a say in his performance and his own life.

What can you do?

Ensuring mental health for athletes who are driven to perform is a complex issue. It is an issue that requires action on many levels. Let us illustrate this with a traffic light. Green, yellow and red.

As mentioned, the vast majority of Danish athletes are doing well. They are the green ones. They should remain there. This requires good environments where young people are not unnecessarily stressed, where they experience coherence and meaning, and where they develop their autonomy. This is an exciting and natural task for any coach.

Some athletes experience real crises, develop an eating disorder, anxiety or depression. These are the reds. They need to be referred to someone who can help. This requires all coaches and managers to know the signs and symptoms to respond to. It also requires that there are clear procedures for referring to specialists and that everyone knows the procedures. Everyone needs to know who to refer to and take responsibility when they see an athlete suffering. When they come back to the sport, they need to be supported. They need a controlled start with a lot of support, just like when an athlete comes back from an ACL injury.

And then there are the yellow ones. These are the athletes who are unhappy – often for a period of time – without it reaching a level where they need a diagnosis or referral to a clinical psychologist. For example, athletes who sleep poorly, are stressed about school or finances, feel a loss of meaning during a prolonged injury period, have not settled in well with a new team, etc. They require special attention. It may be OK to be in the yellow zone for short periods of time, but they need to be helped back into the green and not slip further into the red zone. It is not easy, but overall it is important to show interest, ask questions and create small spaces where they can talk about their challenges and experiences. This could be with their coach, other key people or a sports psychologist.

What do we recommend?

As a coach, you should:

- Show interest in the athletes, not just as athletes, but as people. Ask about their lives and experiences, both in and out of sport.

- Understand the characteristics of good sporting environments that support young people's well-being. You are already doing that, because this book is a great place to start.

- Make sure there is time to recharge. Athletes also need breaks, vacations and socialising. Help athletes understand what actually works for them.

As a manager, you should:

- In collaboration with experts, develop a 'mental health course' that is mandatory for coaches. As a minimum, it should include knowledge about healthy environments, symptoms of mental health problems, mental first aid and procedures for referring athletes who are unwell.

- Keep an eye out. In collaboration with experts, develop a strategy to continuously monitor your athletes' well-being in order to detect athletes in 'yellow' at an early stage. This could be through an annual screening with a questionnaire.

- Ensure clear procedures for how you will deal with athletes in distress, including arrangements with clinical psychologists or other specialists. Such procedures could rightly be developed high up in the system.

Literature

Bissett, J.E., Kroshus, E. & Hebard, S. (2020). Determining the role of sport coaches in promoting athlete mental health: a narrative review and Delphi approach. *BMJ Open Sport & Exercise Medicine,* *6*(1), 1-9.

Henriksen, K., Diment, G. & Kuettel, A. (2023) The Team Denmark applied model of athlete mental health. International Journal of Sport and Exercise Psychology.
DOI: 10.1080/1612197X.2023.2281525

Henriksen, K., Schinke, R., Moesch, K., McCann, S., Parham, W., Larsen, C.H. & Terry, P (2019). Consensus statement on improving the mental health of high performance athletes. *International Journal of Sport and Exercise Psychology*, 1-8. DOI: https://doi.org/10.1080/1612197X.2019.1570473

Kuettel, A. & Larsen, C.H. (2019). Risk and protective factors for mental health in elite athletes: a scoping review. *International Review of Sport and Exercise Psychology.* DOI: 10.1080/1750984X.2019.1689574

Larsen, C.H., Moesch, K., Durand-Bush, N. & Henriksen, K. (2021). *Mental health in elite sport: Applied perspectives from across the globe.* London: Routledge.

Schinke, R., Stambulova, N., Si, G. & Moore, Z.E. (2018). International society of sport psychology position stand: Athletes' mental health, performance, and development. *International Journal of Sport and Exercise Psychology, 16*(6), 622-639. DOI: https://doi.org/10.1080/1612197X.2017.1295557

CHAPTER 6

Foster mental fortitude

We recommend that mental strength training becomes a natural and integrated part of everyday life. Developing young people's physical, technical and tactical strengths is a key part of talent development. The same should apply to mental strength.

Performing in sport requires a high level of technical skill, strength and fitness. Performing under pressure complicates things a bit. Now it is no longer just about skills and form, but also about mental strength. About being able to deliver the same when expectations are high as you can on a good training day.

Let us take the Olympics as an example. For most athletes, success at the Olympics represents the pinnacle of what they dream of achieving. The media attention is greater than ever. The Olympics can be a life-changing event. Success at the Olympics can mean better job opportunities in civilian life, better opportunities for success in the sports career, invitations to popular TV programmes and much more. Athletes bring all of this with them onto the field. In their own experience, they are not only focusing on getting a good performance, but a good life.

Despite athletes being in the best shape of their lives, you see few world records at the Olympics. Why? Because it is hard to perform your very best at this huge event. Because it is a huge challenge to be present in the moment and stay focused on the task at hand when the world around you seems to be going crazy. Because anything can happen, and no matter how well you have prepared, there are no guarantees.

This combination of high importance and high uncertainty is a sure-fire recipe for anxiety.

There are basically two approaches to performing at the biggest events, where the pressure is highest, the opportunities are greatest and the potential consequences of not succeeding are most severe.

One is to treat the Olympics or a championship like any other competition. The athletics track is still 400 metres long, the swimming pool is still 50 metres long, and you still have to go around the marks on the sailing course. The hope is that if you view the championship like any other competition, you will not get too nervous. You 'just' need to think positive and feel confident.

The second approach is to prepare for the Olympics to be the craziest and most chaotic *experience* you have ever had in your sport. Prepare for the fact that even though the course is the same, the experience will not be the same. Prepare for worries, doubts and uncomfortable feelings that you did not expect. Prepare for anything. It requires being open and fully present.

We believe in model number two. There are several reasons for this. Most importantly, in our experience, this is the reality. Even the world's best athletes can be bombarded by irrational negative thoughts before and during a championship. If athletes think they need to be calm, positive and confident to perform, it can really set off a downward spiral when they realise that is not how they feel. At the same time, it is hard to practice for a scenario that only comes up every four years and that few people experience more than once. Last but not least, winning the 'inner' battle – getting your thoughts and emotions under control – is not actually that important. It is much more important to win the outer battle – the battle against other athletes.

The idea that athletes can learn to be okay with whatever comes their way and in turn manage to focus their attention on the task at hand is far more manageable than the idea that they should view the championship as any other competition, think positively and feel confident.

A long way from talent development to the Olympics

However, talent development is not in itself about the Olympics. Few people make it to the Olympics, and in any case, it is something that happens later. So why all this talk about mental strength and major championships here? There are two reasons.

Firstly, athletes' mental strength and approach to performance is established early on. If you teach them early on that they can only perform when they experience full emotional control and high confidence, you are doing them a disservice. They will be vulnerable on competition day if their emotions are out of control. You need to make sure they learn the right lessons from the start.

Secondly, mental strength is one of the factors that sport can provide athletes with. Not all young talents become elite athletes. That is why coaches and managers should want to do something with them that goes beyond medals. Athletes should leave the sport with a backpack full of great experiences and important skills that can benefit them in life. Mental strength can benefit them in a myriad of contexts throughout their lives. We dream that young talents – whether they succeed in their sporting goals or not – will look back and think they gained something important. That they got a better understanding of themselves. That they were equipped as human beings to handle themselves under pressure.

What are the key concepts?

Sports psychology has used many terms that all relate to the mental preparedness of athletes. Attitude, winning mentality, mental toughness, resilience and robustness are just a few. Some of the terms are well-defined, many others are used interchangeably. In this book we use the term mental strength .

We define **mental strength** as the ability to act in line with your values and game plan, even when under pressure and faced with difficult thoughts and emotions.

Mental strength is not about never having to face difficult thoughts and emotions. Mental strength is not about always feeling confident and never having doubts or nervousness. Rather, mental strength is having a clear picture of who you want to be in these difficult situations and being able to act in line with that image.

What do we know?

We know a lot about the psychology behind peak performance and good long-term development. Some of that knowledge comes from research. Other parts of that knowledge come from the work of skilled practitioners supporting top athletes and talents. While neither the research nor the practice experience is clear-cut, here are some of the key insights from the research and from our experience over many years of working in sport psychology.

The mental aspect plays a big role

There is no longer any doubt about the basic fact that the mental aspect is an important part of good talent development and peak performance. You can neither win medals nor fulfil your talent on mental strength alone. You cannot suddenly achieve the impossible on dedication and focus alone. But you can certainly lose competitions and stall in your development when mental strength is lacking.

People under pressure are rarely relaxed

We have experienced many competitions. As athletes, we have participated. As parents, we have watched. As researchers, we have observed. As sports psychology consultants, we have provided support. Many times we have seen how a coach can easily, and with the best of intentions, create unnecessary pressure and doubt in athletes. Creating an unattainable image of mental strength. This happens, for example, when you as a coach say: "There's no need to be nervous, just enjoy it". Or how about: "Just believe in yourself and think you can do it – you'll be fine". When athletes are nervous, struggling to enjoy themselves and experiencing more doubt than belief in themselves, these well-intentioned comments only add to the problem. Not only am I nervous, I'm also 'wrong' and should feel something else in order to perform.

Athletes are not superhuman. They are just people who are really good at their sport. Just like any other human being, they experience doubt and anxiety when they are under pressure. They feel that it's really important to do well in competitions. After all, that is what they train for. This is the time when they need to capitalise on everything they have invested. This is the time to show the world what they can do. At the same time, the outcome is hard to control. After all, the competitors are also training well and trying hard. The combination of high importance and little control is a breeding ground for doubt and concern. It is only natural.

In fact, the struggle to control your thoughts and emotions is causing problems. Think of all the energy athletes have to spend thinking and feeling the right thing. What if they could spend that energy on something more important?

Many athletes find this realisation liberating. When I am competing in a championship, when I have prepared for so long, when it matters so much, when I want it so much, and when I cannot control the outcome, uncomfortable thoughts and nervousness just pop up. It is inevitable. But it is also okay. I do not need to control my thoughts and emotions. I only need to control my attention and my actions. Be fully focused on the task at hand and do the right thing.

Mental strength is in the actions

Although mental strength is mental, it is seen in actions. In principle, it does not matter whether an athlete is nervous or calm, happy or worried during a performance. The key to a great performance is sticking to the plan, doing the right thing and staying focused on the task at hand.

The key for the long jump is high speed, timing the take-off perfectly and floating and landing with good technique – not what he or she is thinking and feeling at the time. A sailor must be in complete control of their course, look out for pressure, hit each wave correctly and always sail the boat with good technique. This requires focus, but it does not require a positive mindset.

And what about a middle-distance runner? A 1500-metre race is intense. There are many interests at stake. Some of the runners on the start line hope for a steady and hard pace. Others fear that scenario and hope for a calm start and a fast finish. The runner never knows how the actual race will play out. This uncertainty creates doubt and discomfort. It can be tempting to do something to reduce the discomfort. The runner could spend a lot of energy telling herself that she is strong. She could decide to run at a certain pace she is comfortable with, no matter what happens. She could look up towards the stands, hoping for a supportive look from the coach. What these actions have in common is that they reduce discomfort. But they also take the focus off the task at hand. To succeed, she needs to be fully present in the race. To be fully focused. To find the courage to make the tactical decisions needed in a split second.

Mental strength can be trained

Mental strength is not something you are born with. It is something you can develop through systematic training. Just like any other skill, it takes real practice. Mental toughness is not something you develop in a single workshop on a Thursday night. It needs to be built into your training, a regular part of your daily routine. It is never too late, but there is no reason to wait either.

Mental toughness training, according to our philosophy, is mainly about training three fundamental processes involved in performing under pressure. The first is the ability to be *in the moment*, to be fully present. The ability to register that your focus sometimes slips. To constantly bring your attention back to the present moment and the task at hand when you notice that it has slipped. The second is the ability to be *in full acceptance*. This is the willingness to embrace everything that comes up, including uncomfortable thoughts, doubts and worries. The understanding that you *are* not your thoughts and feelings, but that thoughts are just thoughts and feelings are just feelings. The last one is the ability to be *in line with your values*. Knowing who you want to be and how you want to perform. Not what result you want, but how. Knowing what you want to stand for, how you want to approach the task. And the ability to act on those values, to return to them every time you lose sight of them.

When athletes train these three skills, they train mental strength. With it, they will be able to perform better – even in an environment where it feels like everything is out of control, including thoughts and emotions. In sports, in exams, in job interviews. And in all the other contexts where they need to hold on to themselves because their thoughts and emotions are running away with them. Therefore, developing mental strength will benefit young people beyond their sport.

Meet Sofie

Sofie is a sailor. Like Thomas in Chapter 2, she is also fictional, but made up of many sailors and other athletes we have met.

When Sofie was very young, she loved sailing. She had not given much thought to what she wanted to do with her sport. There was just nothing better than being on the water, being part of a group of friends and getting better.

At some point, Sofie starts sailing fast. She does well in a few competitions. People around her start to recognise her as a talent. They try to help her structure her training more. She quickly gets hooked on setting goals and milestones. She plans her days. She becomes a master at scheduling. She optimises and it shows in her results. But in all this optimisation, she forgets to enjoy being on the water. In her mind, she is constantly evaluating and planning how to train and improve elements. She forgets the present. After bad training sessions, she gets more upset than good. In a conversation with her coach about values, she realises that the path to happiness is more about being present in the lessons on the water, being a good training buddy and enjoying the community. To focus on development and everything she learns. She is not in a hurry. Sofie embraces these values. She starts practicing mindfulness. She learns to recognise when her mind goes into planning mode and to help bring her attention back to the present moment. On the water, she learns to use her senses, the feel of the water on her face and the waves under the boat, to return to the present moment.

A few years later, Sofie is becoming an established member of the national team. The game has changed a bit. Results are important because they affect her finances and thus how much she can travel to training camps and competitions. Only naturally, she gets caught up in the focus on results. She studies the tables, compares herself to other Danish sailors. She becomes very hard on herself. Even when she makes small mistakes, she often thinks "What am I even doing here when I'm so bad?". She finds that the only acceptable reaction to mistakes and defeat is to beat herself over the head and clearly proclaim that it is not good enough. In this way, she shows that she will not put up with it, that this is not her real level. But it takes a toll on her motivation and well-being. She discusses values with the team's sports psychologist. She is aware of her values. She wants to be goal-oriented, ambitious and development-oriented. Together they realise that these are good values, but something is missing. She has come so far in her career that development happens in very small steps. The others around her are good and will often push her in close situations. To keep up, she has to push her technique so much that mistakes are inevitable. In this reality, it is important to be good to yourself. To be able to recognise your efforts, even if they do not always produce results. To be able to forgive yourself for your mistakes. She does not think this fits with her image of elite sport, but can see that she needs more self-compassion. That value goes on the list.

She starts to train her ability to treat herself as she would treat a good friend who is struggling with adversity.

Now Sofie is at the World Championships. She has been dealing with the mental side of her sport for several years, so she is well prepared. Leading up to the championship, Sofie knows that once she is at the starting line, she will experience doubts and worries and may even paradoxically want to get out. She has been there before. With her sport psychologist, she turns her values around. She wants to show courage. The courage to make decisions, even if there is no guarantee that they are right. She knows what courage looks like in different situations, what characterises a courageous act in a starting situation, when she is behind, when the wind is strong and when the course is difficult to read. She also knows what thoughts often come to visit and can pull her away from her values. During the championship, she is on hard mental work. She often experiences adversity, and each time she registers what is happening, accepts that it feels uncomfortable and returns to the present moment. She reminds herself that she strives to be brave.

When Sofie hung up her wetsuit a few years later to devote herself to work and family, she was grateful for her years in the sport. Not just for the many great experiences, but for everything she learned along the way. Sofie never won the World Championships and did not make it to the Olympics. In that way, she resembles the majority of young talents. But she gained a lot. She learned how to organise trips, how to hold on to a good community in a training group, how to share knowledge with teammates who are also competitors and much more. And she learned how to manage herself. She found out who she is and what values are worth fighting for. She learned that leaning into discomfort in pursuit of what is important can be exciting. She developed mental strength.

What can you do?

Many coaches feel better equipped to manage the physical, technical and tactical parts of training, and it is easy to forget about the mental aspect.

But the mental part takes up a lot of space for athletes. Not spending time on the mental part is like telling young people that it is not important, or even that they are 'wrong' if they cannot handle that part themselves.

This is not to say that all young athletes need a sports psychologist. Far from it. Overall, we want mental strength training to become a much more integrated and natural part of everyday life for young talents. It must be incorporated into daily training. Coaches should not be sports psychology consultants, but they should be comfortable working with simple forms of mental training. They must be comfortable with the fact that the mental aspect is a natural part of the dialogue with the athletes.

What do we recommend?

You can do this as a leader:

- Ensure that coaches are trained to have a dialogue about mental aspects of life as an athlete.

- Collaborate with a sports psychology consultant, who especially supports the *coach* in working on the mental aspects. With young athletes it is rarely necessary for the sports psychology consultant to have individual sessions with the athletes.

- Invite elite athletes to talk about the mental challenges they experience and how they deal with them. Help these role models not fall into the trap of painting an unrealistic picture of eternal confidence and inner peace, but instead deliver an honest account of performance anxiety and bumps in the road.

You can do this as a coach:

- Spend time helping young people discover who they want to be. Expand the daily dialogue to include conversations about values and meaning. What do young people want the next generation of young athletes to learn by watching them? What would they be proud of people saying about the way they achieved or failed to achieve their goals?

- Play with value-driven actions in everyday life. Bring small cards to practice with simple value words such as 'supportive', 'curious' or 'brave'. Let the athletes choose a card and let them practice living the value during an exercise. Afterwards, talk to them about what was difficult or easy, when they forgot the value and what it meant to their experience.

- Do simple mindfulness exercises, for example before training. Help athletes to be fully present in the moment, to register any thoughts and feelings that arise and to slowly bring their attention back to what they are doing.

Literature

Henriksen, K. (2019). The values compass: Helping athletes act in accordance with their values through functional analysis. Journal of Sport Psychology in Action, 10(4), 199-207. DOI: 10.1080/21520704.2018.1549637.

Henriksen, K., Hansen, J. & Larsen, C.H. (Eds.) (2020), Mindfulness and acceptance in sport: How to help athletes perform and thrive under pressure. London: Routledge.

Henriksen, K., Storm, L.K., Stambulova, N., Pyrdol, N. & Larsen, C.H. (2019). Successful and less successful interventions with youth and senior athletes: Insights from expert sport psychology practitioners. Journal of Clinical Sport Psychology, 13(1), 72-94. DOI: 10.1123/jcsp.2017-0005.

Knight, C., Harwood, C. & Gould, D. (Eds.) (2017). Sport psychology for young athletes. London: Routledge.

Part 2

Sustainable talent pathways

In the book's foundation, the talent philosophy, in Chapter 1, we established that children are not little adults. We are not in a hurry. The goal of talent development is to create athletes who can perform at the highest international senior level, not just produce good youth results. We argued that when you slow down, let kids explore multiple sports, let them fail and play, and design competitions that encourage slow learning rather than fast results, you support their long-term development and opportunity to be great.

In the second part of the book, we substantiate our claims about the talent philosophy and focus on the paths to the world's elite. We will present research-based knowledge and give concrete recommendations on how you can work with talent identification, specialisation and talent transfer, and we will dive into which types of training really work.

Remember, a philosophy only comes to life when it is put into practice.

CHAPTER 7

Foster many, cut few

We recommend that talent developers focus on talent development rather than talent identification. It is hard to spot talent at an early age and all too often you get it wrong. Therefore, you should identify and select as little as possible until after puberty.

Talent identification has become a natural part of youth sports. Imagine a normal spring day at the local football club. A large group of excited young boys and girls have arrived for the club's first training session of the season. Full of anticipation, they set about practicing the sport they love. Peter is their coach. He looks them over, assesses. Who should play on the A team, the B team, etc. Whether he is aware of it or not, Peter is identifying and selecting talent.

When Peter spends time and energy on identifying the most talented players early on, it is because he understands talent in a certain way. He sees talent as something that is innate, that only a few have and that predicts later success. Only athletes with the right conditions can reach the world's elite. This understanding comes naturally to Peter.

Talent identification is tempting. Imagine if Peter can see in advance which of the young players have a chance of becoming really good, true world stars. Then he can avoid spending time and resources on helping players who are not going to win medals anyway. And the young people who lack talent do not have to invest blood, sweat and tears in a project that is doomed from the start. Or is it?

Identifying and selecting talent has consequences. Young people who are not considered talented can have their dreams crushed. Conversely, the young people who are touted as the next big star can experience stress and pressure of expectations. We have seen families get so caught up in their son or daughter's talent that they forget to be a family. And we have seen groups of friends being torn apart when children or youngsters cannot train together.

Considering the implications, you may be asking yourself if there is any evidence for early talent identification at all. We take a closer look.

What are the key concepts?

Spotting, recruitment, identification, selection, etc. Let us first grasp the most important terms and definitions. There is not complete agreement on the definitions, so let us offer some clarification here.

Talent recruitment is the systematic search for young people with the right 'gifts' to become great at a sport they do not yet play.

Talent identification describes finding the athletes within a given sport who have the greatest potential to become elite athletes. In most sporting environments, some degree of talent identification takes place as coaches assess which of their athletes they believe in the most.

Talent selection is the step that follows identification. It happens, for example, when a manager at a sports academy selects applicants for their few coveted spots, or when the swimming coach has to choose who can join the talent team, which only has a few lanes in the swimming pool.

Talent selection can be done in several ways:

- **Natural selection** happens 'by itself' and is present in every sport. As children get older, some will continue to play sport and some will not. Some youngsters who used to play multiple sports will choose to focus on one. Natural selection is *appropriate* when young people choose to quit because their interests change. It is *inappropriate* when young people choose to quit for all the wrong reasons, for example, because they feel that the coach does not believe in them or because they are being pressured to train much more than they want to.

- **Active strategic selection**, on the other hand, is when a club or coach actively selects some athletes over others for specific teams or talent pools. In a *systematic scientific approach,* athletes are tested for strength, technique, size, endurance, etc. In a *tacit knowledge approach,* on the other hand, the coach will select athletes from a holistic assessment based on their 'eye for talent'.

What do we know?

A lot of research has been done into talent identification. In recent years, researchers have let the numbers speak for themselves: talent identification is difficult and often wrong. But researchers have not been as successful in explaining *why* it is so difficult and *how* best to work with identification and selection.

We therefore decided to team up with Claus Hansen. Handball is a big and prominent sport in Denmark and Europe. Denmark is a powerhouse in international handball, and Claus has long been a central figure in Danish handball. He has devoted his life to handball and has been a vital and visible part of virtually all the talent initiatives that time and again have kept Danish handball's talent development world-class. National youth coach, assistant national coach, league coach, academy teacher, coach education teacher – Claus has done it all.

We have known Claus for many years. He is outgoing and curious, and most of our meetings have been on his initiative. He has called us when he wanted to hear about new research findings or discuss an idea. This time it was our turn to reach out to him. In the shadow of the corona pandemic, we invite him to a Zoom meeting. When we state our purpose, a talk about talent, Claus begins by saying that time will tell. His point is that today's talented handball players are a product of something that happened 10-15 years ago, and that it will take many years before you can see if what you do today has actually worked.

Talent identification is difficult

Researchers have clearly shown that talent identification is fundamentally difficult. Quite simply, it is hard to predict who will be the next Lionel Messi or Michael Phelps. Talent identification is difficult for many reasons. First, talent is composed of many dimensions. What is most important? The right height, the right parents, the right attitude? Athletes have different strengths and must compensate for different weaknesses. Second, 'taste' and fashion are of great importance. Which traits and playing styles are in fashion? You judge talent based on what it takes to win today. But you do not know what it will take to win in the future, when young talent hits the big stage. Third, when you look at young people, you see skills, not potential. There is often a big difference in how much help young people have received. An athlete may have more potential than their teammate who currently has better skills. This is because biological maturity varies from person to person. Finally, when testing talent, the results show not only talent, but also how well the person handles being tested.

A good illustration of how difficult it is to identify talent comes when you look at when certain talents are born. It is said that it was a Canadian psychologist, Roger Barnsley, who first noticed a peculiar pattern in the mid-1980s. He discovered it by accident during a game with the local ice hockey team. Before the game started, he and his wife were looking at the game programme listing the team's players. His wife noticed a pattern that no one else had noticed: the vast majority of the players were born in the first three months of the year. It was remarkable. Roger was curious, and when he got home, he started looking at other club teams, national teams and other sports. The conclusion was striking. The phenomenon was everywhere.

The phenomenon has since been dubbed the *relative age effect*. The effect simply describes the fact that on a sports team there is an overrepresentation of athletes born in the first part of the selection year. Why is this? Let us return to Peter, the youth coach we introduced earlier in the chapter.

Peter is watching the young footballers and has to select players for the first team, the talent centre or the academy. Peter sees one of the young boys who is clearly ahead of the others and identifies him as a special talent. In reality, the player is just a little older and has been training a little longer than the others on the team. Now Peter gives the selected player more attention and support and better training conditions. With the extra training, the small difference becomes a bigger difference and suddenly the older player is further ahead.

In 1997, researchers were given the perfect opportunity to test the hypothesis when FIFA (the international football federation) decided that everyone should compete in years divided from January 1 to December 31. In Belgium, the selection year had previously followed the school year starting in August. Now comparisons could be made and the results spoke for themselves. Whereas young Belgian footballers previously had the best chance of being selected if they were born between August and October, players now had the best chance of being selected if they were born in January, February or March.

Today, researchers have examined the relative age effect across sports and countries. The conclusion is clear. The relative age effect is a common phenomenon in all sports where people compete in age groups.

Claus Hansen has been interested in the phenomenon for many years. He clearly remembers the realisation when, as a youth national coach during a tournament in Hungary in 2012, he discovered that Denmark had almost exclusively players from year 94, even though the tournament was for both year 94 and 95. That is when Claus decided to do something about it. We will get back to that.

We get it wrong far too often

You have probably seen it happen. A really talented young athlete did not make it. He or she suddenly lost interest, perhaps due to an injury, or maybe their development stalled and they were simply left behind. Perhaps you have also experienced a talented athlete appearing 'out of the blue'? An athlete who was not initially identified as talented, perhaps because she was too small, too unfocused in training or just not good enough. But suddenly she has taken a huge leap because she has grown or because she has made a choice to focus on her sport.

These experiences correspond well with what the research shows. Arne Güllich has been researching the effectiveness of talent identification and development programmes for many years. He and his colleagues have recently reviewed and compiled the research, both their own and that of others. They initially examined 20 national talent identification and development systems, seven national sports federations in several sports, more than 1,000 football players in German U15-U19 teams and 600 Bundesliga players, more than 1,500 selected athletes in Olympic sports, 39 elite sports schools and 246 clubs in various sports. In other words, the basis for the research results is solid.

We are familiar with the research, but still contact Arne to see if there is any new knowledge in this area. Arne is from Northern Germany. He has spent several summers on the west coast of Denmark and loves Denmark. So he was excited when we contacted him and even more excited when we asked him about his new projects. Arne is a nerd in a good way. Together with good colleagues, he has spent the last few years diving into even more studies with the desire to gather the many studies into a single systematic overview. The research is growing all the time, and he says that he now has so much data that they can say something more precise about individual sports and not just in general. The results are just around the corner, he says. That is why we invite him to Denmark, where he will give a presentation to all of Team Denmark's sports managers.

Arne exudes a nice mix of warm enthusiasm and cool insight. He remembers the numbers and knows exactly what conclusions to draw.

First, he highlights that early identification is not a prerequisite for success. Athletes who made a select team in youth, but did not make the national team were often identified and selected early, while world-class athletes were selected later. Across Olympic sports, for example, they found that the best senior athletes were generally selected for national teams and Olympic training centres two years later than those who 'only' made the national elite. The numbers vary only slightly and the trend is consistent across all sports.

Secondly, he highlights a clear trend of 'first in, first out'. The younger athletes are when they enter a talent programme, the younger they are when they leave. Across the many talent programmes and projects included in Arne Güllich's research, the likelihood of being in a talent programme after five years was only five per cent. Arne looked specifically at German football. Even when statistically adjusting for the fact that some players move from one academy to another, 29 per cent of players are replaced annually. After five years, this means that just under 20 per cent of the original players are still in a football academy. Those who make it the furthest have come in later.

In other words, most good juniors do not make good seniors. Most good seniors were not good as juniors. Arne's numbers are based on such large data sets that we dare to use the old phrase "numbers don't lie".

Talent developer Claus Hansen, who we mentioned earlier, recognises this from handball. He explains how the best senior players are not actually those who were selected early. The relative age effect is almost reversed by the time athletes reach the senior elite, and Claus sees many born in December among the best. But why is that?

Early selection is the first step on the wrong path

During Arne's talk, one of the coaches asks why the athletes selected early do not become the best? After all, they get to be part of the best early on. Unfortunately, part of the answer is that the selected athletes are often selected for training organised in ways that do not lead to international success. In other words, it is about what happens once an athlete is selected. Here, Arne explained that they had compared the training history of athletes who were selected for talent programmes at age 14 or younger with athletes who were selected at age 15 or older. Not surprisingly, the research showed that the athletes selected early started specialised training earlier, they started competing earlier, they reported much more intensive training at an early age and they played fewer sports than the athletes selected late. At the same time, the athletes selected early suffered more injuries and achieved great results in junior championships, but rarely achieved international senior results.

These results show that the athletes selected early are subjected to highly uniform and deliberate practice. As we will discuss in the next chapter, this is not the optimal path to the world elite.

Claus Hansen sees the same thing in handball. He exudes clear frustration when he says that the selected players are being exploited. They play many matches and many minutes in each match. The players maturing early simply get injured more often and are worn out both physically and mentally. At the same time, they are not given the opportunity to develop all facets of their game. Instead, they are forced to utilise only a few strengths, which wins games in youth handball, but not in the senior ranks. Claus gives an example where a coach made a strong player force through and score whenever he had the opportunity. The team won many games that way, and the player was seen as a big star. But by the time the player became a senior, the opponents had gotten bigger and faster, and there was much less room to power his way through. Since he had never practiced shooting from the outside, opponents knew he was always trying to force his way through. This made him easy to stop. Soon after, he was outperformed by a player who not only had one strength, but also had developed different skills towards his senior years.

What are the consequences?

Yes, it is difficult and yes, you are often wrong, but sometimes you get it right when you identify and select young people based on their talent. So why is it so problematic?

- *It destroys communities.* The other day we were watching a group of 10-12-year old boys playing football in a schoolyard. The sun was shining and even though it was cold, they had shed their jackets. Some of the boys were big, some smaller, but they made it work and the atmosphere was intense and concentrated with lots of laughter. We enjoyed the sight because we love the ability of sport to stimulate play and community. After a few games, it was time to form new teams. Two captains were selected and had to take turns to choose. As few remained to be selected, we heard someone say: "If we take one A player, you get two B players". We saw that their A and B team identities had moved into the schoolyard. It was a little painful to watch. Talent selection can lead to friendship groups being broken up.

- *Talent is being left behind.* What about all those who do not make the cut? We showed earlier how athletes who are not initially identified as talented later move past the selected ones and win a spot on the national team. These athletes have stayed motivated and kept training even though they were not viewed as talented. But there are also athletes who lose motivation for a sport when they sense that the coach does not believe in them. For example, athletes born at the end of the year.

- *It creates an unfortunate self-perception.* What does it do to young people when they get a talent stamp on their forehead? Some grow with the task, but evidence suggests that for some young people it can have unfortunate consequences. For some, it leads to perceived pressure of expectations and excessive perfectionism and self-criticism. Growth mindset research also suggests that talented people who are told they are good *because* they are innately talented are more likely to give up when faced with adversity.

Here too, Claus Hansen's experiences support the research. In addition to the fact that the early bloomers are pressured to play a lot and therefore suffer many injuries, he has a suggestion as to why it is often the late-maturing players who are best in the long run. They have had to fight harder for it. The many small defeats have given them resilience. They have had to improve their technical and tactical skills even more to compensate for their physical deficiencies. Ok, so this sounds good, but Claus Hansen is worried. How many potentially talented athletes never gave the sport a real chance because they lacked recognition and were never selected?

However, Claus points out that the biggest impact may not be about the individual players at all. The trend is towards centralisation, where the best players are gathered in the strongest clubs. This affects everyone. The strongest players find it difficult to be matched in matches, and the less strong players are overmatched. Then you see matches ending 40-10, and that is no fun for anyone.

So why do people identify talent?

The research speaks for itself. Talent identification and selection is an unfortunate strategy. Yet it still happens all the time. We ask Claus why, and he has many good suggestions:

- Firstly, the motives are different. Club coaches understand that the federation is concerned with developing talented players for the senior national team, but they will often say that their job is to win games. They play matches every week, and it is on the basis of the results of these matches that coaches gain recognition and can advance to better coaching jobs. The tournament structure, where teams can move up or down, certainly does not help either. According to Claus, it only encourages coaches to focus even more on results rather than development.

- Secondly, Claus mentions parents and increased mobility. Parents care about their children winning. They put pressure on coaches and are quick to change clubs if results are disappointing.

And then we get to the root of the problem. Players become hostage to the agenda of the coach and parents. When a coach is struggling to win youth games, he knows that the recipe is to field the strongest team and focus on a few key players, namely the early bloomers. Unfortunately, the recipe for good long-term talent development is quite different.

What can you do?

During Arne Güllich's visit, the Danish sports managers listened intently to his presentation of data. Convinced of the validity, they now turned their attention to the solutions. What do we do? Research has generally been better at identifying problems than developing creative solutions. Although Arne makes his living from research, he also emphasises that pointing to the problem is not enough. Arne's research and Claus' experience together provide some ideas.

First of all, both Claus and Arne would like large clubs to set a clear agenda with a focus on development, so that individual youth coaches are not so easily seduced by personal ambitions to win matches and competitions. Clubs and academies need to focus much more on learning and development and much less on competition. After all, athletes spend far more time in training than in competition, so it is during training that the primary development takes place. And it does not help that the best coaches only work with the best players. The best coaches need to engage with many more young athletes. For example, they need to go to competitions with all the athletes. It is no good if the best coach always accompanies the best team. That is actually the easiest task, and then you send an inexperienced coach with the team that needs much more help, as it consists of athletes who can potentially and develop a lot more.

All young people should feel seen and that they are part of one big community in practice. The same applies to matches and competition. There can be different levels, but everyone should try their hand at competition equally.

Claus also suggests rethinking why you select players. When he was a youth national team coach, he did away with the classic idea that a youth national team should be run like a club team, where you select the strongest players and aim to win matches. Instead of 22 players, he invited 35 to the national team gatherings. He gave the players the benefit of the doubt. He describes how after a successful tournament, he selected a completely different national team for the next tournament, a team that consisted mainly of younger and late-maturing players. This gave the first national team players time to develop in their clubs and gave many more the chance to experience the international level. The young team actually did well. He proudly says that many of the players who joined in the second round are still playing handball and that several of them form the core of Denmark's successful men's national team.

The relative age effect is a chapter in itself, and Claus has done a lot to counteract it. He has held coaching seminars. He has told the story that the late bloomers often end up as the best. He has influenced clubs and academies to look at players' birth dates when selecting teams. Claus says he was inspired by a Canadian study and during an observation event, he gave all the fourth-quarter kids a neon green headband. This way, when observing the youngsters, the coaches were reminded that a smaller player might not be able to keep up, but that he was also just a little younger. It actually changed who they selected. It is the same idea behind many football nations' Futures Teams, which are special national teams for athletes born at the end of the year.

What do we recommend?

- Drop talent identification and selection or wait as long as possible, at least until after puberty.

- Keep an open mind if you are identifying and selecting anyway. Look for potential for long-term development rather than current skills.

- Combat the relative age effect, for example by reserving a number of spots for athletes born at the end of the year.

- Make sure talent programmes are 'porous' so that athletes who are late developers or late to dedicate themselves to one sport can still find their way in.

Literature

Cobley, J., Baker, J. & Schorer, B.W. (2020). Talent identification and development in sport (2nd edition). London: Routledge.

Güllich, A. (2014). Selection, de-selection and progression in German football talent promotion. European journal of sport science, 14(6), 530-537.

Güllich, A., Barth, M., Hambrick, D. Z., & Macnamara, B. N. (2023). Participation patterns in talent development in youth sports. Frontiers in Sports and Active Living, 5, 1175718.

Güllich, A. & Cobley, S. (2017). On the efficacy of talent identification and talent development programs. In: J. Baker, S. Cobley & N. Wattie (Eds.), Routledge Handbook of Talent Identification and Development in Sport (1st edition, pp. 80-98). London: Routledge.

Güllich, A. & Emrich, E. (2012). Considering long-term sustainability in the development of world class success. European Journal of Sport Science, 14(S1), S383-S397. DOI: 10.1080/17461391.2012.706320.

CHAPTER 8

Allow for ample avenues to the world elite

Recently, we had the pleasure of talking to the manager of a tennis club. He had experience from other sports and was concerned about what he saw among young tennis players. Among other things, he told us that the youngsters trained a lot and almost always with a paid personal trainer on the other side of the net. He hardly ever saw two of the young players meeting on their own initiative and playing with each other. He said that among the parents there was an extreme focus on the volume of training. He was never met with suggestions for new fun activities for the children, but was constantly asked to make more practice sessions. He very rarely heard laughter from the courts. He had a vision of something different and more. A great environment for children and young people with a focus on play, where training varied and where young people took the initiative to play tennis themselves much more often. But at the same time, he wanted to create an elite. He wanted to create a club that created winners. Some parents called him a dreamer. He asked us if that was a completely unrealistic ambition. "You're onto something," we could reassure him. "More than you know."

Developing from talent to elite athlete undoubtedly requires many hours of training. This is hardly a surprise. To become good at anything, you have to practice. But how you practice and the quality of the practice matters. There is good evidence that broad and versatile training in the early years forms the basis for long-term and sustainable elite sport. In Denmark, physical education in schools is organised as a broad introduction to many sports, and for many years we have had a tradition that the vast majority of children in their younger years try out different sports in local clubs. This is called 'sampling', or early diversification.

Today, however, we are seeing a trend of athletes getting serious about their sports at an earlier age. They are training very purposefully much earlier. This worries us.

We recommend that you as a talent developer create opportunities and open up many different paths to the elite. Make space for versatile development and for the talent's own free initiative. It is your responsibility as a professional to create the foundation for a long-term development path for the talents, rather than creating success in terms of results 'here and now'.

In the pursuit of the 'promised land', the big contracts and international recognition, it is easy to believe that the earlier children get started with targeted and intensive training in a specific sport, the better. This has become a 'truth' in some parts of youth sport, which is paradoxical because there is actually evidence to the contrary. This is particularly highlighted by the last decade of empirical studies and a number of solid scientific reviews of the overall literature.

What are the key concepts?

The pathways to the elite are shaped by several building blocks. The foundation is, as mentioned in chapter 1, the talent philosophy, but in many ways also the context, for example the culture and traditions of a particular sport and the culture of Denmark in general. These are the building blocks, four of which are particularly important:

1. when to start playing sports and your primary sport

2. whether you play multiple sports along the way

3. at what age you join talent programmes

4. how much play, deliberate practice and competition, respectively, take up the training in the sports you play.

These building blocks of sport specialisation can be put together in many different ways. For example, you can see young people who only play one sport, but on their own initiative play a lot in their sport. Or young people who train very purposefully and compete a lot, but in multiple sports.

Early specialisation is defined as a child playing only one sport, or at least primarily one sport, from an early age and being part of a targeted training programme, such as a talent programme, from the age of 5-12. The child has a large volume of training and high-intensity training in that sport throughout childhood, and tournaments, matches and participation in leagues take up a considerable amount of time.

Early diversification, also known as *sampling*, is defined as the child engaging in multiple sports throughout childhood in both formal and informal settings and only later specialising in one primary sport. This also includes the concept of *intra-sport diversification*, which covers the opportunities to try out and practice other sporting activities organised *within* the primary sport. For example, handball training may be supplemented with hockey, but organised within the handball club.

Early focus is defined as a child starting early in their primary sport, but without practicing large volumes or with very high intensity throughout childhood.

Deliberate practice means demanding and structured training *activity* with the goal of improving performance through specific exercises. It is a form of training designed to optimise the athlete's skills. It is not necessarily fun and therefore requires motivation and persistence.

Deliberate play is a form of activity that can be done with minimal equipment, in non-specialised facilities, with any number of players of different ages and sizes, and without the need for an adult to organise it. Examples are roller hockey in the neighbourhood or football on the city's multi-sports field. This type of training gives freedom to try out and play with different movements and tactics. It creates the opportunity to learn to improvise and develop your understanding of the game.

Coach-organised **playful training** is a type of activity that does not require specialised facilities. This type of training is organised and guided by a coach and can be organised with any number of players of different ages and levels. The coach adjusts the environment and lets the game itself be the teacher.

What do we know?

There is a consensus that the path to the world's elite involves large volumes of intensive training. But when this should be and how it should be organised is much more nuanced. We know that there are several different paths to the world's elite, but that does not mean they are all equally good. Some paths are both more likely to succeed and more sustainable than others.

Arne Güllich's new analysis of hundreds of international studies and thousands of athletes, which we mentioned in chapter 7, speaks volumes. World-class athletes play multiple sports throughout childhood and adolescence.

More precisely, the analyses show that world-class adult athletes have played more sports in childhood and adolescence, started in their primary sport later, accumulated fewer training hours in their primary sport in the early years, and even developed more slowly than athletes who 'only' reached the national elite level. This pattern is clear. And it is not essential that the other sports the athletes played were similar to the one they ended up becoming world-class in. It is the very act of learning from other sports.

The analyses also show that athletes who were best as youth athletes, but did not reach the world elite level as seniors started playing their primary sport earlier, trained more at a young age, were more focused on one sport, and had faster initial progress than those who reached the senior world elite.

How can this pattern be explained? We cannot know for sure, but three solid suggestions have been put forward as possible explanations. The first is based on a *sustainability logic*. When children specialise early, there is an increased tendency for them to get injured and burn out. Injuries and burnout are easier to avoid when you are less busy trying to reach the world elite. The second explanation is the good *match between person and sport*. When children specialise in one sport at an early age, they simply risk choosing the wrong one. That the sport does not match the person's physique, temperament, preferences and talent. Conversely, when the child is allowed to try multiple sports, he or she is more likely to make the right choice later on. The third explanation is about the *transfer of learning*. According to this explanation, varied physical experiences and learning in the early years of sport are an important prerequisite for the more specific learning needed later on.

Talent development in Scandinavian

In our efforts to get a handle on the pathways to the world elite and understand what is special about Danish and Scandinavian talent development, we turned to one of the Swedish researchers who has been looking at this topic for decades, Per Göran Fahlström, or PG for short. PG is currently employed at Linnaeus University in Sweden, and he has 35 years of experience as a badminton coach. He has been everything from children's coach to national coach. He is also a person with a big heart for research into talent development, especially research that is close to practice and can be translated into strategies at national federation level. His research has always found its way directly to the Swedish national coaches.

Throughout his working life, PG has had a special interest in the development of Swedish elite athletes and their different paths to the national team and the top of the world. We reached out to PG because he has followed the research field over several decades and is committed to putting knowledge into practice.

PG's research shows that Swedish national team athletes often come from sporting families, with a high proportion having parents who have coached, managed or played sport at a high level. In general, athletes have played at least two different sports other than the one they end up playing. By the age of 15, they choose their main sport and focus on it, and a year later they start to focus on becoming really good. Overall, the studies show that the pathways to national team level are many and individual, but also that the Scandinavian sports model is largely characterised by sport sampling in childhood and later commitment.

Particularly in relation to team sports, PG says that athletes at the highest professional level often started in childhood, but were involved in other activities alongside their primary sport. Often other team sports. He also says, with concern in his voice, that today he sees a tendency for the youngest athletes to specialise earlier and earlier. We will come back to that in a moment.

Research into the pathways to the world elite started in the US, and data now comes from much of the Western world. But our cultures are different, and what works in one place may not necessarily work in another. Therefore, it is important to emphasise that PG, we and other researchers have studied specialisation pathways specifically among Scandinavian athletes. The primary pathways in our neck of the woods are four.

1. *Early specialisation* is the path where athletes focus on a sport early on, invest in it and prioritise the performance aspect. They have large amounts of deliberate, targeted training throughout the specialisation pathway. By 'investment' we mean that they prioritise the sport over other activities.

2. *Early focus on one sport, playful training and late investment* is the path where athletes focus on one sport early on, although some 'taste'

other sports, but they prioritise social aspects of the sport in the early years and experience training as fun. Only later, they commit to the sport.

3. *Early multi-faceted sporting practice, playful training and late investment* is the way in which athletes in their early years of sport *play* multiple sports. There are even some who have 'talent' in multiple sports. Nevertheless, they prioritise social aspects in the early years and experience training as fun. Only later do they choose one primary sport and invest in it.

4. *Late entry into primary sport* is the path where athletes start late at the age of 15 or older in the sport they later become elite athletes in. As a result, their specialisation process is relatively compressed and they invest from the start. The athletes often have experience of training hard and purposefully from previous sports activities.

Of course, part of it is about the traditions of the sports. Triathletes may start as adults, while talents in football, ice hockey and gymnastics may have started as children. But the overall conclusions cut across sporting cultural divides.

Heading in a wrong direction?

So, we know from numerous studies that sampling is not only associated with an increased chance of reaching the elite, but also increases the breadth of motor skills, makes it more likely to choose correctly and reduces the risk of injury. Quite simply, there is evidence to avoid early specialisation. In our conversation, PG asks: "Why build our Scandinavian system around early specialisation when it's unnecessary and can have negative consequences? Sport systems would be wise to keep creating opportunities for many different pathways." But that is not what he sees. He talks about analyses he did based on data from 325 Swedish national team athletes. He divided the group into the relatively youngest athletes on one side and the relatively oldest athletes on the other. He looked for differences. He found that there were more variations of late specialisation among the relatively oldest and more variations of early specialisation among the youngest. There was a tendency for the youngest national team athletes to have played fewer different sports during childhood and to have focused on just one sport earlier. PG sees this as a sign that we are moving in the wrong direction. He believes that the analyses basically show that this is the path currently available.

PG is concerned about the picture he sees where parents, in addition to the club or academy's good offerings, buy extra training from private providers. PG asks who has an overview of the total training load? He finds that these parents strive for rapid development in their dream of their children reaching the world elite. They may achieve great youth performance, but they are at increased risk of injury and dropping out. At the same time, the trend of buying extra private training creates increased inequality and economic bias. In Scandinavia, we value the fact that everyone has equal opportunities to become skilled.

Vicor Axelsen is the greatest badminton player in the world. When he came back from the Tokyo Olympics with a gold medal he used his platform to warn against this trend, specifically aimed at ambitious parents: "My fear is that more and more parents will try to take control of their children's training too early, and it will become too serious too early. The most important thing for my parents was that I liked playing badminton and that I thought it was fun. I'm not sure I would have fallen in love with the game if my parents had 'paced' me to have four private training sessions a week at the age of seven, eight or nine".

What can you do?

The latest and most solid evidence tells us that early diversification develops a broader foundation of cognitive and motor skills, carries less risk of injury and is more likely to lead to a senior elite career than early specialisation.

Therefore, no system should encourage children to specialise early. But that is not to say that children should not play organised sports at an early age. They can. But it should *not* be combined with early intensive and uniform training. The easy access to organised sport from a young age, in our view, places a special ethical responsibility on the shoulders of child coaches and club leaders.

The big task for you as a talent developer is to customise the training so it makes sense for the young people you are coaching. Do they play one sport intensively? Are they doing one sport supplemented with other activities? Or are they in a place right now where they are engaging in multiple sports, only to favour one later on. Either way, you should think about how to ensure they all develop a broad base. In addition, we also recommend keeping a keen eye on societal trends. When playing ball games for fun at recess is replaced by social media, you might want to consider whether you can create a framework for this kind of play in your training.

What do we recommend?

- Calm down, calm down. Do not be seduced by youthful achievements. Believe you have plenty of time.

- Focus on the quality of the workout rather than the quantity.

- Make room for training activities that do not have a one-sided and short-term focus, but are organised with a long-term perspective. Remember, when striving for a broad base, you cannot expect early success.

- Support talents to do activities on their own where they can experiment. This has a positive impact on the talent's sense of autonomy and influence, which creates long-term motivation. It requires you to create space in the programme.

- Strategise to create a broad base. This is partly about supporting young people to participate in multiple sports throughout childhood and early adolescence. It is also about ensuring variety within the sport, for example by integrating exercises and elements from other sports. Finally, you can change the training space, for example, by inviting swimmers into open water or organising a beach football tournament.

- From the age of 15, targeted training is ramped up. The next long period requires motivation and perseverance. That is why it is important that you do not run out of mental resources, hunger, commitment and focus during childhood sports.

Literature

Barth, M., Güllich, A., Macnamara, B.N. & Hambrick, D.Z. (2022) Predictors of Junior Versus Senior Elite Performance are Opposite: A Systematic Review and Meta-Analysis of Participation Patterns. Sports Med 52, 1399-1416. DOI: 10.1007/s40279-021-01625-4

Fahlström, P.G., Gerrevall, P., Glemne, M. & Linnér, S. (2015). Vägarna till landslaget : Om svenska elitidrottarens idrottsval och specialisering [Pathways to the national team: On Swedish elite athletes' specialization]Report for the Swedish Sport Confederation

Ford, P.R. & Williams, M.A. (2017). Sport Activity in Childhood. Early specialization and diversification. In: Baker, Cobley, Schorer, & Wattie (Eds.). Routledge Handbook of Talent Identification and Development in Sport (1st ed.). London: Routledge. DOI: 10.4324/9781315668017

Güllich, A., Macnamara, B.N. & Hambrick, D.Z. (2022). What Makes a Champion? Early Multidisciplinary Practice, Not Early Specialization, Predicts World-Class Performance. Perspectives on psychological science : a journal of the Association for

Psychological Science, 17(1), 6-29. DOI:
10.1177/1745691620974772

Storm, L. K., Henriksen, K. & Christensen, M. K. (2012). Specialization
pathways among elite Danish athletes: A look at the
developmental model of sport participation from a cultural
perspective. International Journal of Sport Psychology, 43(3),
199-222.

Güllich, A., Barth, M., Hambrick, D. Z., & Macnamara, B. N. (2023).
Participation patterns in talent development in youth sports.
Frontiers in Sports and Active Living, 5, 1175718.

CHAPTER 9

Tolerate talent transfer

At the 2020 Tokyo Olympics, Primož Roglič, a Slovenian cyclist and former ski jumper, stood at the top of the podium in the road cycling time trial. He began his sporting career as a ski jumper at the age of eight, became the Junior World Team Champion in ski jumping in 2007 and has won other prestigious competitions in ski jumping. But in 2011, he decided to swap his skis for a bike and embark on a new career. He started as an amateur in 2012 in Slovenia. He turned professional in 2016 and quickly caught the public's attention with impressive results. The following year he took part in his first Tour de France and won a stage. In 2018, he won the Tour de Romandie and finished fourth in the Tour de France. In 2019, he repeated his Tour de Romandie victory. Has three consecutive wins in the Vuelta a España. Today, Primož is among the absolute world elite in cycling.

Examples of athletes switching paths can be seen all over the world, including in Denmark. In lightweight double sculls, rower Anne Lolk and Juliane Elander finished fourth at the 2012 London Olympics and ninth at the 2016 Rio Olympics. Before she started rowing, Anne was a four-time world champion in the K2 marathon kayak. The two rowers started their collaboration ahead of the 2012 London Olympics. Anne was new to rowing, but not to elite sport. Juliane was an experienced rower. Together they would retrain Anne from kayaking to rowing.

Ida Karstoft practically sprinted from the football field and straight into the athletics stadium. Most Danes know Ida as the smiling girl who participated in the 2020 Tokyo Olympics as part of the Danish 4x100 metre relay team on the athletics track. We also know her as the holder of the Danish 200-metre record. But not everyone knows that Ida was an accomplished football player and actually made her debut for the national team before she swapped her football boots for spikes.

These are all examples of unique career paths and how even elite athletes can change paths.

There is great potential in creating opportunities to change paths. This can benefit the individual athlete who has lost motivation for their primary sport, but not for playing sport in general and for training purposefully. But it can be just as beneficial for the sport to invest strategically in talent transfer, especially in small countries like Denmark.

Research in this area is still sparse and in its infancy.

What are the key concepts?

In the previous chapter, we introduced the concept of sampling. It describes athletes playing multiple sports before choosing their primary sport. Research has shown that world-class athletes can benefit from playing multiple sports in their early years. Sampling should not be confused with talent transfer, which happens later.

Talent transfer describes when an athlete who is already at a high level in one sport switches to another sport and achieves a high level in the new sport.

Structured talent transfer is a formalised and structured process for switching sports. It consists of identifying and selecting athletes who are already skilled in one sport and helping them to a higher level of success in another sport. In the context of talent transfer, 'donor sport' refers to the first sport in which athletes achieve high levels and 'transfer sport' refers to the sport in which the athlete subsequently achieves elite status.

Successful talent transfer is defined as an athlete who achieves high-level performance, for example, competing at national or even international level in both their donor sport and their transfer sport. It also includes youth athletes.

What do we know?

Internationally, there are only a few studies of talent transfer, but there is plenty of inspiration to be found. A group of British researchers led by Professor Dave Collins looked at data from athletes who participated in the 2010 Winter Olympics and 2012 Summer Olympics. They wanted to get an overview of how often talent transfer occurs and investigate the mechanisms behind it.

Talent transfer is surprisingly common

First and foremost, the researchers found that many Olympic athletes have switched paths. A surprising number of athletes had been elite in one sport and made it to the Olympics in another.

The researchers examined profiles of 2,307 athletes from the UK, Australia, USA and Canada, through publicly available web pages. They were reviewed for information on the athlete's background prior to involvement in either the 2012 Summer Olympics or the 2010 Winter Olympics.

The UK and Australia have invested heavily in formal national talent transfer programmes. The US and Canada do not invest in formally structured talent transfer in the same way.

At the Summer Olympics, 38 out of 541, or seven per cent, of Olympic athletes on the Great Britain team had undergone a successful talent transfer. This was defined in this study as athletes who had previously been at an elite international or national level in one sport and were now at the Olympics in a new one. In comparison, it was five per cent for Australia, six per cent for the USA and five per cent of athletes on the Canadian team.

Looking at the Winter Olympics, an even higher proportion of athletes had a successful talent transfer. On the Australian team, it was 13 out of 49 athletes. On the Great Britain team, it was 15 out of 52. That's just around a quarter of all Australian and British athletes. The numbers were somewhat lower for the USA and Canada, but still just around ten per cent. All in all, a significant proportion of athletes. We were surprised by these high numbers.

The study cannot explain the differences between countries. In our view, that is not the most interesting thing either. What is interesting is that so many Olympic athletes have changed paths in their careers. These are not just one-off unique stories. This is a real pathway to the world's elite.

Collins' study also looked at other interesting questions, including which sports are most commonly switched from and to, and at what age. In the study, there were actually 177 different combinations of donor and transfer sports. This is surprisingly high considering there were 15 different sports represented at the Winter Olympics and 39 sports represented at the Summer Olympics.

There were some sports that were more often part of the pattern than others. For example, athletics (sprinting) was by far the most frequent donor sport, but football and basketball were also frequent donor sports. When it comes to transfer sports, bobsleigh was the most frequent. This is probably due to the fact that there has been a large-scale effort in England to actively recruit athletes for bobsleigh from other sports, which the statistics reflected. The sprinting disciplines of athletics, rowing and skiing were also sports that often welcomed former elite athletes and created sporting success.

Changing paths is undoubtedly not only an issue for established elite athletes, but also for young people. Overall, the results reflected that there are many and varied career paths. The age of talent transfer ranged from as young as 11 to as old as 32, but about half switched sports between the ages of 16 and 21. This might indicate an ideal age to focus on talent transfer.

Similarity between sports is not essential

It is only natural to ask why athletes who have achieved a high level in one sport can reach elite level in another. After all, they lack several years of training in the new sport and should therefore lack too far behind. What explains their success?

A common assumption is that it requires similarities between the two sports, primarily technical, tactical and physical similarities. A good example is the transfer from sprinting on the athletics track to bobsleigh – the same explosive sprint out of the starting block is required to bring the sled up to speed. The Danish Sailing Association has been discussing the possibility of recruiting gymnasts to crew the 49er boat. The 49er is a lively boat that requires the crew to be fast, strong and have phenomenal balance. That description fits a gymnast well. In these examples, the focus is on similarities in physical and motor skills between the sports.

But physiology is not everything. There are more mechanisms at play. The literature highlights the transfer of attitude, habits and psychological skills as important mechanisms in successful talent transfer. When a young athlete has been in a talent programme in swimming, gymnastics, football or another sport for several years, there is a good chance that they have learned to be goal-oriented, to find motivation – even in the tough times – to deal with adversity and defeat, to evaluate constructively, to engage positively in a training community and much more. These are all psychosocial skills that mean they will be able to develop significantly faster in a new sport.

In the UK, sports organisations work very purposefully and systematically with talent transfer programmes. Their experience is that it is not enough to focus on physical and motor skill similarities that coaches often take as their point of departure. Their research shows that it is beneficial to focus more on behavioural and psychological skills.

What can you do?

Although research in this area is sparse, we believe that the idea of talent transfer can open up more and new pathways to the elite. Pathways that can be valuable for athletes and federations alike. We recommend that the established systems open up opportunities to switch between sports. Primarily for the benefit of the individual athlete.

We see talent transfer as something that is not only relevant when working with elite athletes, but also earlier in their sporting careers.

Are we sure that people leaving one sport do not want to use their mental and physical skills in another? Who is looking at that question? We believe that every young athlete who wants to leave their sport should be offered the opportunity to test themselves in a new sport. Think of a talented 17-year-old football player who finds his development stagnating and motivation disappearing. There is no longer room at the academy and he does not play other sports because football has taken over his life. Who will talk to him about what other sport he can use his skills in? Who takes responsibility for creating the opportunities? Maybe he could become a good runner? Maybe the athletics club a few kilometres away could be the setting for a new adventure in his life with sports. Just like it happened for Ida Karstoft. Or what about the swimmer who loves to train and compete and loves the serious lifestyle, but realises she does not have the right physique to reach her goals? What happens to her when she stops? Probably not much. Could she achieve her sporting ambitions in another sport with the right help?

This requires understanding that the similarities between donor and transfer sports can be an advantage, but are not a prerequisite for a successful switch. In some cases, something completely different can be beneficial precisely because the athlete's physique or physiology was not suited to the donor sport.

Athletes can undoubtedly benefit from their genetics. Fast muscle fibres, height, etc. But also their psychological characteristics, which, according to researchers, play a crucial role in talent transfer. It is about being able to learn quickly, being persistent through the transition and having high motivation to test themselves in the new sport. The psychological skills are universal and do not require similarities between sports.

It is also about organisations such as federations, clubs, academies and associations making an effort to deliver and receive athletes in an efficient and supportive way. That they see it as a process they need to support. With the right reception, training and patience, new opportunities can open up. But do you see them?

What do we recommend?

- Cultivate an interdisciplinary dialogue about the possibilities of allowing talent transfer. For a moment, set aside self-interests and look at the bigger picture. Which sports could you benefit from working with, to the benefit of the individual athletes and the sport in general?

- Recognise the donor sport when an athlete achieves great results in a 'new sport'. This makes it easier for a sport to support athletes who want to switch.

- If you are in a position to do so, think laterally. The coach at the football club naturally thinks about football, just as the swimming club thinks about swimming. But someone should take a strategic approach to talent transfer. A strategy could include an annual talent festival where young people can try new sports, or a targeted conversation with all young people at a certain level who quit their sport.

Talent transfer creates the opportunity for environments to renew themselves, especially if you have the courage to use the experiences and perspectives that 'new' athletes bring to the environment. Talking to young people about what they have learned in previous sports and being inspired by that.

It requires more collaboration and less rivalry.

Literature

Collins, R., Collins, D., MacNamara, A. & Jones, M. I. (2014). Change of plans: an evaluation of the effectiveness and underlying mechanisms of successful talent transfer. Journal of Sports Sciences, 32:17, 1621-1630, DOI: 10.1080/02640414.2014.908324.

Pion, J., Teunissen, J.W., Ter Welle, S., Spruijtenburg, G., Faber, I.R. & Lenoir, M. (2020). How similarities and differences between sports lead to talent transfer: A process approach. In: Blaker, Cobley & Schorer, Talent Identification and Development in Sport: International Perspectives (2nd edition). London: Routledge.

Van Harten, K., Bool, K., van Vlijmen, J. & Elferink-Gemser, M (2021). Talent transfer: A systematic review. Current Issues in Sport Science (CISS), 6, 006. DOI: 10.36950/2021ciss006.

CHAPTER 10

Facilitate fruitful feedback

We recommend that you, as a talent developer, play more with the organisation of training. Change the environment and let the environment provide feedback that encourages athletes to develop creative solutions. In general, use feedback more flexibly. Feedback can be given in many different ways and have different effects.

Recently, we had scheduled an interview with a talented young ice hockey coach. We were to meet at the ice rink, but got there early and had about two hours to get a feel for the club and how training went. That afternoon and evening, several teams were practising. In the rink, there were players aged from about 15 and all the way up to the league team.

The first thing we noticed was how similar the training sessions looked across age groups. The warm-up consisted of the same elements. Many of the same exercises were included in the training. When they played a match towards the end, it was also hard to tell the difference. The size of the rink, the number of players, the puck. It was all the same. One of the youth coaches was talking to a player on the side line. We went over and asked if what we were seeing was unusual. Both the coach and the player laughed a little and said that they considered it a very normal evening.

We paid extra attention to the coaches' way of using feedback. Here, too, we saw a similar pattern. The coaches were good at correcting mistakes. They had a good eye for which mistakes were problematic. They were not afraid to stop the game or pull a player aside and give a good tip. But we also noticed that their feedback was very similar. They mainly gave feedback on tactics, such as "You should have passed earlier" and technique, such as "Remember to carry the stick all the way through the movement". Their feedback was about eliminating mistakes and doing things right. We got a clear impression that there was one right way and many wrong ways. We also noticed that feedback was something coaches gave to players. We neither saw players giving feedback to the coach nor to each other.

The coach we had come to talk to is a league coach. In other words, he coaches the best senior players. We asked him what he particularly wants in the players he brings into his team. He was in no doubt. They need to be good at making decisions. Good at analysing the game and adapting if the tactics are not working. They need to be creative and brave. They have to take responsibility on the ice. They have to lift the team. He laughed and said he knew it was a tall order. "The club has many players who are physically strong and technically skilled. But there are not that many creative and courageous players."

We wondered if there was a connection. Whether the coach's way of organising the training and giving feedback also gave the players good conditions for training creativity and courage. Or whether the players were actually being trained to be more concerned with being correct than creative, safe than brave.

We discussed our thoughts with the coach. His first natural reaction was to defend the club and the coaches. We had to understand that flawless technique was also important. Without it, creativity did not matter. Then he was quiet for a while until he said that this was something they needed to talk about among the coaching staff.

What are the key concepts?

Basically, we use the term feedback to refer to systematic feedback to a person about their behaviour. It can be about their performance, behaviour, contribution to the team, club etc. In sport, feedback is often something a coach gives to an athlete, but can easily occur from athletes to coaches, between athletes, between coaches etc. Feedback is often, but far from always, verbal, as you will see examples of in a moment.

What do we know?

A lot of research has been done on training. From a macro perspective, research has been done on how and how much an athlete trains throughout their career. We wrote about this in chapter 8. We clearly showed that there are many paths to world class, but also that there is no rush and that specialisation at an early age is not an advantage. From a micro perspective, where the focus is on the individual training session, research has been done on pedagogy and didactics, the pros and cons of different types of training, individual learning styles, the importance of group dynamics for learning and much more. In the following, we will focus on a crucial factor in accelerating learning: feedback.

When the environment provides feedback

Duarte Araújo is a researcher at the University of Lisbon. His passion is to push the way we think about training. Together with a group of international researchers, he works with what he calls an 'ecological constraints-based approach'. This means that he focuses on the natural constraints of the environment and how coaches can develop athletes by manipulating and changing them.

Duarte believes that all too often training yields too little benefit. When you, as a coach, put your athletes through the same exercises and practise the same movements over and over again in the exact same setting in order to eliminate errors, you are training the athletes' ability to do just that. To perform a specific skill under those conditions and with few errors.

This kind of training may make young athletes perform well at an earlier stage, but not in the long term. And is this smart? Is it the skill that athletes need to develop into elite athletes and perform at the highest level? Not according to Duarte.

Close your eyes for a moment and imagine a complete contrast. Imagine the beach where Marta, female football star and five-time FIFA Player of the Year winner, learned to play. It is a stretch of beach on the outskirts of a city in Brazil. A river flows through the beach and a large traffic bridge crosses it. This is where Marta grew up as a football player. Some days she played against other girls and was much better than them. Other days she played against boys and had to work hard. At some times of the day, it was quiet and the players could easily talk to each other. At other times, there was traffic noise and players had to find other ways to communicate. Some days the sand was light and dry, other days wet, heavy and slow. Some days the pitch was large, other days the river overflowed its banks and made the pitch smaller. At some times, the sun was high in the sky and the heat was suffocating. At others, the sun was low and blinding on the horizon. Here Marta learned not just to play football, but to be creative, to adapt to changing conditions and to come up with new strategies.

In other words, Duarte suggests that you, as a coach, should instruct and error correct a little less. Instead, you should change the environment and let the environment provide feedback to your athletes. As an ice hockey coach, when you put loud music on in the rink, you force players to use silent communication more. When you change the court size as a badminton coach, you force players to focus on the elements of their game that fit the new size. As a football coach, limiting the number of touches forces players to pass earlier. As a boxing coach, when you change the distance to the bag, you force your fighter to try new foot positions.

Duarte's point is not that silent communication is better than speech in ice hockey, that some shots are better than others in badminton, that football players hold the ball too much, or that boxers should stand differently in relation to the bag. His point, however, is that it is important to train the ability to adapt. Why? Because elite sport is never simple and rarely runs smoothly. Football pitches vary in size. Other teams create tactics to catch your team off guard. Some opponents in boxing have longer arms than others. In other words, analysing what is happening and developing and implementing a new strategy is crucial in many sports. That is why you should train this skill.

Do not tell players that you are going to change this and that to train their ability to do this and that. Let the environment provide feedback. Let the players realise that what they are doing might not be optimal. Let them come up with ideas. Let them train their ability to analyse and adapt.

When the coach gives feedback

Coach feedback plays a crucial role in driving development and peak performance. Useful feedback is about more than supplementing criticism with praise. A few years ago, one of us was asked to write a chapter on feedback in elite sports for a book on feedback. It quickly became clear to us while working on that book that it would be exciting to involve a coach who has mastered the noble art of feedback. Someone who does it every day. So we contacted Peter Hansen, who was a national coach in Olympic sailing and has coached sailors who have won medals at the European Championships, World Championships and Olympics. We had seen Peter in action and particularly liked his sense of feedback. Together we developed a model for good feedback in sailing.

Sailing is a complex sport. Many factors play a role in a sailor's performance, including tactics, strategy, technique, gear and physique. These factors are also not always equally important because the weather changes. The simple fact is that sometimes races are won by starting well and having good speed, sometimes by having a superior tactical overview and sometimes by being able to handle difficult waves. In the type of boat Peter coaches, there are two sailors on board. Peter cannot communicate with the sailors while sailing. This means that on the water, Peter often only has the opportunity to talk to the sailors just before the start and during the short breaks between each race. On a busy race day with several Danish boats in action, this means short conversations lasting two to three minutes, hampered by wind noise. Peter's feedback strikes a delicate balance between helping sailors perform optimally and empowering them to make good choices.

In our conversations, we agree that feedback has several functions, but that the most important one is to direct the athletes' focus. As a coach, you do this by giving feedback on some things over others. As Peter sits in the coach's boat on the way out to the course, he makes many observations. He observes the degree of mast bend, how the sails twist, the speed of the boat, the position of the sailors in the boat, the sailors' manoeuvres, and he observes how the wind is acting. At the same time, Peter has to measure the current and wind. Before the start, the sailors approach Peter. Now he has to make a number of choices. Which areas should he give them feedback on? What kind of feedback?

Peter's choice of feedback is important for sailors' focus. Imagine that Peter gives a short instruction on the setup, for example that they need to tighten the mainsheet a bit more, and then asks about the tactics, for example where on the course the sailors have observed pressure. The sailors automatically look out over the course and in their mind's eye they see a way around the course. Imagine, on the other hand, that Peter gives a short comment on the tactics, for example that the course seems open, and instead asks about the technique, perhaps how best to sail strongly in this type of wave. Then the sailors will see in their mind's eye how they work to get the boat to hit each wave correctly. So, as you can imagine, Peter can use his feedback to partially control where the sailors' attention is and what they are talking about.

As we talk about examples from Peter's years of experience, it becomes clear to us that we can divide feedback into four main types.

- *Confirmation* is all about giving sailors *confidence*. By pointing out that a particular element is under control, it gives athletes a basic sense of security and confidence, while opening up the door for them to focus on something else that's more important. For example, Peter will tell a crew that their trim is spot on.

- *Instruction* is often about *correcting a detail*. As a coach, you may need to correct a specific technical detail. For example, Peter might tell a crew to stand a little further back on the boat because the waves will stop them less.

- *Observations* have the purpose of *directing focus* without providing answers. When Peter shares an observation, for example that the Germans' boat is flatter on the water and that they are sailing fast, he directs the athletes' focus to certain basic sub-elements, the ones he believes are crucial in today's practice or competition.

- *Questions* create *reflection and autonomy*. When Peter asks questions, he puts his sailors in a position to analyse and reflect on their technique or tactics and make their own decisions. For example, Peter might ask the sailors what options they have to make the boat lose less speed in crab waves, or what is especially important to get a good start in jumping winds.

These forms of feedback are not equally relevant in all situations. During an important competition with performance targets and time pressure, Peter's overriding goal is for the sailors to deliver top performance. This means that Peter's feedback will generally focus on what he believes is crucial to winning the day's races, not on the crew's development goals. When under time pressure, he will often choose confirmation or instruction as a form of feedback because sailors need quick solutions. It is quite different on a good hot training day, where the goal is development and there is plenty of time for reflection. Here, the sailors develop insight and understanding that enables them to win in the long term. Peter's choice of feedback will be based on the crew's development focus in the given period. Peter will often choose observations and questions as a form because they encourage the sailors to think for themselves, make decisions and test solutions.

In practice, the coach will often use several forms of feedback at the same time. It is a pleasure to watch Peter juggle good feedback when he is at his best. When he has four or five boats on the water and he is navigating between the sailors in his lightning-fast coaching boat. One of the crews is absolutely world-class, another is relatively new. And then there are those in between. The course is the same, the weather is the same, but the athletes are very different. To one crew, Peter says: "Your sailing setup is great. Did you notice which side of the course came up to the top mark first?". Peter confirms the technique and directs the crew's attention to a tactical element. To the next crew, Peter says: "You must dare to continue further out on the edge. With the wind we have today, what is crucial for you to keep the boat flat and at high speed?". Here it is the other way around. We have asked Peter many times how he decides what kind of feedback to give. Sometimes he can explain it, sometimes he cannot. As with so much other expertise, Peter often makes his choices quickly and based on tacit knowledge.

When athletes give each other feedback

Coach feedback to athletes is important. However, in the best environments, it does not stand alone. In the best environments, there is a culture of feedback between athletes. Athletes train together, compete against each other and know each other's strengths and weaknesses really well. The best environments are characterised by openness. Here, athletes contribute to each other's development by giving each other feedback.

Peter emphasises this in his story. He knows that a significant part of his success lies not in his own feedback, but in his ability to create a feedback culture *between his sailors*. His sailors give each other feedback and make each other better, even if they are competitors. They do this based on the idea that the better our training partners are, the better we become.

Danish sailors have been raised to be autonomous and to take responsibility. Peter has no doubt that this autonomy is a contributing factor to their success. This is mainly due to the fact that the sailors often train without a coach present. The sailors spend much of the year travelling and the coach is not always with them. In other words, they need to be able to improve without Peter's feedback. They do this partly by analysing their own sailing and development, and partly by having a strong training group where feedback flows freely. Especially from the best sailors to the young lions and lionesses reaching for the experienced ones' place on the podium.

It works. In our own research into successful talent environments, role models have proven to be an important feature. In all the great environments we have studied, role models are close by. There is an exchange of knowledge. The experienced ones give feedback. When we ask what this means, young people say that the experienced eye is invaluable. The experienced ones say that they gain a lot from analysing, reflecting on and communicating what they actually do to succeed.

What can you do?

It takes a determined effort to create an environment characterised by lots of good feedback, but it is not impossible to achieve. In our opinion, it is worth the effort.

For many years, it has been difficult to increase the training volume of athletes. They train as much as they can handle. That is why the motto has been 'train smarter, not harder'. There are many roads to Rome and many roads to good, effective training. Our suggestion is that it pays off in practice to turbo-charge learning and give feedback that has traction.

What do we recommend?

- Rethink your training. Do you tend to organise workouts so that they often contain the same elements? So there is little variation? So there are a lot of repetitions? Then consider whether you can use the training environment more actively. If you can create constraints in the environment that force your athletes to develop new solutions, to train their adaptability.

- Talk to the coach at the level above the athletes you train. The coach you dream of delivering great athletes to. Ask them what they want your athletes to be able to do when they move up a level. Then look at your training. Are you mainly training skills that athletes need to perform at their current level? Or are you actually developing the skills that athletes will need in the near future?

- Take a look at your feedback. You know the most common challenges, the ones you comment on most often. Write a confirmation, an instruction, an observation and a question for each of them. Consider when you will use which type of feedback. Play with different scenarios. Ask athletes what they need and when.

- Create a culture of feedback between athletes. Train them to give each other feedback. Ask the young ones to ask the experienced ones when they are struggling with something. Let the experienced athletes know that you need their help. Say many times that the better the training competitors on the team are, the better we all become.

Literature

Araújo, D., Davids, K. & Renshaw, I. (2020). Cognition, emotion and action in sport: An ecological dynamics perspective. Handbook of sport psychology. Hoboken: John Wiley & Sons,

Davids, K., Araújo, D., Vilar, L., Renshaw, I. & Pinder, R. (2013). An ecological dynamics approach to skill acquisition: Implications for development of talent in sport. Talent Development and Excellence 5 (1), 21-34.

Henriksen, K., Knight, C. & Araújo, D. (2020). Talent Development Environments. In: Hackfort & Schinke (Eds.). The Routledge International Encyclopedia of Sport and Exercise Psychology. London: Routledge.

Part 3

Holistic talent development environments

In the foundation of the book, the talent philosophy, in chapter 1 we argued that a strong and cohesive environment is a prerequisite for strong individuals. Not just the training environment, but the entire environment.

Some environments are simply better than others at nurturing and developing elite athletes. We emphasised the importance of context, role models and meaningful relationships. We argued that in a context characterised by high ambitions for socially responsible talent development it makes sense to shift the focus from talented athletes to talented development environments.

In the third part of the book, we focus on the good talent development environment. We will present research-based knowledge and provide concrete recommendations on how to enable meaningful relationships, work strategically with role models and engage in dialogue with schools and parents.

Remember, a philosophy only comes to life when put into practice.

CHAPTER 11

Cultivate caring connections

Top athletes have had many different people in their lives who have had a significant impact on their learning and development. Some have been with them all the way, others for shorter periods of time. Some cross the athlete's path and pass by without making an impact, while others make a significant impact by pushing the athlete in a completely new direction. Important skills in life and sport are learned and developed in relationships, which is why it is relevant to consider them in talent development.

We recommend that you nurture the quality of your own relationship with the talent, but, just as importantly, help them open their social horizons and learn from others.

We first noticed this in one of our previous research projects, where we interviewed Danish elite athletes about their career paths. By chance, we found a pattern in the relationships that had been career-defining. Here we show an example with a sailor.

She was interviewed at home in her living room. With great commitment, she talked about all her experiences in sailing at different stages of her career. She talked about the people who had influenced her development. As she talks, she draws significant events on a timeline, where she also marks the ups and downs.

She details an incident from her teenage years where a passing relationship pushed her career in a new direction. She had very good youth results in her boat class and envisioned herself continuing in that class for many years. At the same time, she met a coach who encouraged her to switch to a different type of boat. He told her that there was an opportunity to compete in a Youth World Championship that acted almost like a mini-Olympics. He thought she would do well, that the new type of boat would suit her well. Now, suddenly and almost randomly, she was faced with a possible switch between two boat types. She had a lot of doubts. Her father, who she listened to a lot, did not think it was a good idea. Nevertheless, she decided to make the switch. The next few months were tough. The work to increase physical strength and weight was as hard and demanding as it was necessary to succeed in the new boat. The results did not materialise. Doubt was a frequent visitor. Still, she persevered and won a medal at the Youth World Championships. It was a highlight for her that opened many doors.

It was exciting for us as researchers to hear. A single piece of advice from a coach with a high degree of legitimacy changed her career trajectory and laid a foundation for her later success.

She also talked about another crucial relationship with another coach who followed her closely over many years: "She had a very special impact on me," she said, elaborating: "...in the way I developed my approach to life and my way of thinking in training and competition. She taught me how to make the best of every situation. She has made a big difference to me in the way I have developed as a sailor and as a person."

Before we get back to what is at the heart of the sailor's two different types of relationships with two coaches, let's get clear on what an influential relationship actually is.

What are the key concepts?

Influential relationships are relationships that have been so significant that athletes, in their own words, "wouldn't have made it without them". These are relationships that are crucial for learning and development, which have prepared the athlete to make important choices and master particular transitions in their career. When athletes look back on their careers, key relationships are described as a fundamental part of their success.

Influential relationships that create opportunities are often short-term relationships that initiate a transition or shift in career. It is a gatekeeper.

Influential relationships that create meaning are long-lasting and have an existential importance for talent. It is a partner.

What do we know?

For many years, research has mapped *who is* important for talent development and when. That is, the focus has been on the people – parents, coaches, peers – and their roles at different points in time. For example, research has shown that parents are key in the early years, but their importance diminishes as athletes get older. Later in life, teammates and the athlete's partner become central. In other words, the focus has been on the people rather than the relationships.

There are different types of relationships

We found that the relationships themselves were crucial. All athletes looked back on their careers and were able to identify key relationships they would never have succeeded without. At the same time, we found a clear pattern across many elite athletes' narratives. They described different types of relationships. Some relationships created opportunities, others created meaning. Some relationships helped push the athlete in a new and unexpected direction, and others were deep relationships that influenced the talent's formation, identity and life values. Both types of relationships were crucial.

One type is influential relationships that *create opportunities*. They initiate a transition or shift in your career. They provide direction and influence career choices. The relationship is built on a high level of trust in people with a high degree of legitimacy. They can be short-term acquaintances, but have a decisive impact. The sailor above is a good example. She has a relationship with a coach. The relationship is short-lived but ends up being crucial because it pushes her in a new direction. The right direction. It was not until later in her career that the sailor realised how important this relationship had been in her development.

The second type is influential relationships that *create meaning*. Meaningful relationships are long-lasting and have an existential importance for the talent, who is not only learning technical, tactical, physical and mental skills, but is very much in the process of forming as a human being. Some relationships go beyond the sporting context. In our interviews, we heard examples where the relationship with a school teacher or a music teacher was crucial to the sporting talent's life values. Others 'pull threads' across phases of their career. This could be a relationship with a coach from their youth that is significant throughout their career. Some athletes talked about how they still sought advice from a former youth coach late in their adult career. Others talked about how they had a special coach with them as an inner voice that still guided them.

Relationships that create meaning were described as personal, deep and long-lasting relationships that were significant. They provided ongoing existential support that influenced what was meaningful in the athletes' lives. They had a decisive influence on the athletes' life values and philosophy of life.

Just think about the other coaching relationship that the sailor above described. She talked about a coach who was *crucial to her approach to life* and the way she developed as a sailor.

What can you do?

We see two different types of relationships. They are both essential. One is not more important than the other. They complement each other. And many athletes, when they look back on their career, can point to both types.

As a talent developer, you are probably concerned with developing good relationships with your athletes. Hopefully, you are visible as a role model and care about the talent as people, not just athletes. This is important. But the work does not stop there.

Enabling meaningful relationships also requires you, as a talent developer, to help build meaningful relationships with people other than yourself. This means giving up influence and control. After all, you have no control over the direction in which other key relationships may guide your athletes. But it is important that they have access to multiple relationships.

We recommend that talent development environments provide opportunities for talent to cultivate more relationships, gain new inspiration and maintain important relationships with others outside the environment. This is fundamentally much more important than having complete control.

What do we recommend?

- Talk to talent about who matters and what they mean.

- Encourage talents to seek out dialogue with other coaches and people from domains other than sport.

- Empower young talent to maintain long-term relationships throughout their careers.

- Be very aware of your own legitimacy when giving career advice. Talent has a special ear for certain people. Especially if you are a national coach or otherwise have a special status, you need to be conscientious and not take young people's questions lightly.

Literature

Storm, L.K., Henriksen, K., Larsen, C.H. & Christensen, M. (2014). Influential relationships as contexts of learning and becoming elite: Athletes' retrospective interpretations. International Journal of Sports Science & Coaching, 9(6), 1341-1356. DOI: 10.1260/1747-9541.9.6.1341.

Skrubbeltrang, L.S., Olesen, J.S., & Nielsen, J.C. (2022) The coach as gatekeeper, distributor of resources and partner for sports talents, Sports Coaching Review, 11:2, 233-251, DOI: 10.1080/21640629.2021.1978730

Dohsten, J., Barker-Ruchti, N. & Lindgren, E.C. (2020). Caring as sustainable coaching in elite athletics: benefits and challenges. Sports Coaching Review, 9:1, 48-70, DOI: 10.1080/21640629.2018.1558896.

CHAPTER 12

Reward responsible role models

We recommend that talent developers work consciously with role models in good talent environments. We all know the value of someone to look up to, to learn from. As a general rule, good role models do not just happen. It takes active work. But it is worth the effort.

Danish badminton enjoys great international success and their work with role models is a key part of the recipe. One spring day, we had the opportunity to observe the Danish badminton players' training. The atmosphere was full of energy and inspiration. One impression stood out in particular.

Viktor Axelsen was one of the participants in the training. It was incredible to see him in the technical exercises. Sometimes it was him doing the training and one of his teammates setting up for him. At other times, it was Viktor in the role of the feeder. You could not tell the difference if you were not paying attention. Viktor was as concentrated and involved when he was in the setter role as when he was on himself. And the younger players just soaked it up.

It is obvious that the role of the feeder is crucial to the quality of technical training in badminton. If the shuttles are not placed accurately, you cannot practise your shot with sufficient quality. It is also obvious that it is more motivating for the individual player to train themselves than to be the feeder. This creates a dilemma. Here, Viktor led and showed the way. He had decided to be the world's best feeder. The key here, however, is not Viktor's role as a trainer, but his role as a role model. With his impressive track record, commitment and focused approach, Viktor was a clear role model for young players. The young players wanted to be like him. Therefore, they, like Viktor, made an effort to be fully focused in their role as feeders. This improved the overall quality of the whole squad's training.

What are the key concepts?

It is important to have someone to look up to. But role models can take different forms.

A **master** is a role that is primarily described in literature on apprenticeships in skilled trades. Research has nicely demonstrated how a lot of learning can take place in contexts where there is no actual teaching. This happens when an apprentice follows an experienced master craftsman and mimics their approach to tasks.

A **mentor** is an agreed role. This role exists in many contexts. In good environments at universities that facilitate elite athletes to take an education under special conditions, it is not uncommon for an older fellow student to be responsible for helping a new athlete find their footing in daily life. Sometimes the mentor even receives a token payment.

An **idol** describes someone whose success can inspire others. Classic examples are music stars, actors and sports stars.

A **role model** is close by and may, for example, be the slightly older athletes in the talent community. They show what it takes. They demonstrate concrete exercises, show a training mentality and take the time to talk to young people. They create culture by leading the way in everyday life.

What do we know?

It is well-established knowledge in social psychology that role models play a key role in young people's identity development. We have known this for many years. We also know that sport plays a major role in young people's identity development, at least for ambitious talents. Therefore, it is surprising that there are only a few studies in sports psychology that have specifically examined role models.

But do not despair. We can learn from studies of good talent development environments. We clearly remember our first studies of selected talent environments in Scandinavia. We followed the environments over time, interviewed athletes and coaches. And we observed many hours of training. We saw elite athletes organise training for the younger ones and demonstrate exercises. We saw elite athletes explaining to a younger athlete over a recovery drink how they planned the week and ensured recharging. We saw elite athletes leading the way with a smile on their way into the toughest elements of training. It struck us again and again how crucial role models were in the environment.

Role models need to be close by

Everyone needs someone to learn from. Neither sporting nor personal skill development takes place in a vacuum. Young athletes need role models in their acquisition of concrete skills and even more so in their development of a training mentality. They need to learn how to be an athlete, how to manage their talent.

Role models need to be physically close by. Role models need to be present in the training environment to make a difference. Not every day, not all the time, but not infrequently either. It is not enough for them to give a lecture once a year or send a video greeting at an award show. It must be possible for young people to observe them, imitate them, ask questions, ask them for advice and guidance.

It should be easy to identify with role models. The more the role models resemble the young talent, the more the young people believe they can achieve their goals by being inspired by the role models. A 12-year-old novice track and field athlete who does not yet know whether she wants to run, jump or throw has a hard time learning from a national javelin thrower. She has to learn from the 14-year-olds, who in turn have to learn from the older members of the talent squad, who in turn have to learn from the national team.

Role models learn something too. Older elite athletes find it meaningful to 'give back to the sport'. But they also emphasise that they themselves learn something from being role models. When young people ask questions, they are forced to self-reflect. They are forced to consider what they have actually done to become good, what values they want to stand for. When a sailor is asked how she sets trim in waves, it makes her think about something that is otherwise habitual or tacit knowledge. This reflection, elite athletes tell us, can be worth its weight in gold. At the same time, it is a positive affirmation of their position in the community. It is simply great to be the one that others look up to.

Role models are not only other athletes in the same sport. Role models can also be older siblings, a coach, athletes in other sports or others who lead the way.

Evidence suggests that athletes prefer role models who are more than athletes. Today's young athletes do not look up to elite athletes whose entire identity is based on their performance. They prefer role models who also stand up for their beliefs and values in life. They prefer role models who are able to combine good performance with a good life.

Same same, but different

Working with role models is a hallmark of all good talent development environments, but our case studies have also shown that it can look very different in different environments.

In the Danish sailing community, they have a formula for it. Our top sailors training for the Olympics have the next generation on the water with them every day. The elite needs someone to train with and compete against. They need someone to sail alongside, so they can see if small changes in trim or setup make the boat faster. Young people need someone to learn from. Young people are allowed to participate in training sessions, sit in on daily evaluation meetings. They take over equipment. They ask questions. In many ways, elite athletes act as coaches. The young people say they learn much more than technique and tactics. They learn how to plan, organise, book flights and apartments. They learn to set goals for training and to change them when the wind blows more or less than they expected. They learn to take responsibility.

In a Swedish athletics environment, the elite and the talent group trained daily at the same time and in the same hall, however with separate coaches. When the young talents had to learn a new exercise, it was not uncommon for one of the elite athletes to be asked to demonstrate. At the same time, one day a month the elite athletes were responsible for training the talents, who in turn were responsible for training the younger athletes below them on another day of the month. The talents said that the most important thing they learned was to be fully present in training. To be focused.

In a Canadian trampoline environment, the hall was set up in such a way that you could not help but see world-class jumpers training on a daily basis. The young talents saw how the elite invited skilled jumpers from all over the world to come and train. They learned not only to jump, but also to be open and curious, to share knowledge, to reach out for international inspiration.

In several football environments, we have seen how it is part of the first team players' contracts that they can be asked to help out as assistant coaches on the youth teams. They are asked to do this if, for example, they are injured and unable to train.

The list of examples is long. The message is clear. Role models play a crucial role in the development of young talent.

In 2014, we investigated a golf environment that, despite good resources in terms of finances, facilities and well-trained coaches, had not succeeded in developing a professional player, even though that was the academy's stated goal. They contacted us because they wanted us to look at their environment and point out where they could improve. When we compared the environment to our studies of highly successful environments, a number of differences stood out. One of them was about role models. The young players at the school had no access to good role models. There were talented senior players in the region, but the young talents did not meet them. The senior players seemed to have no interest in training with the talents. Once in a while they were on the course at the same time, but there was no dialogue, not even a greeting. And they never followed each other around. It was a challenge. The young players had many questions about scheduling how many other sports they could play alongside golf, finances and sponsors. The young talents missed the informal dialogue with someone who was just a few steps ahead. Today, the Danish national golf team is very focused on role models, with Danish pro players leading the way at training camps and mentoring younger players.

What can you do?

As a coach and manager, you are often tempted by more structure. You think you can increase the quality of training by dividing athletes into groups and ensuring that young people train with someone at their own level. That is why you create age and level groups. But good role models do not come by themselves. As a talent developer, you must make an effort to create good conditions for cross-cultural dialogue. Open communities across age and level may be difficult, but they also open up the magical possibility that learning suddenly occurs, even when you are not teaching.

Elite athletes find their careers meaningful when it is about more than results. They grow and develop by giving back, by being there for the next generation.

Young talent needs someone to look up to. They grow and develop when they see that the best also fail, that they also struggle sometimes, but that they do not give up. When they see that the best share knowledge, open up and are curious. When they see that the best also train the elements of the sport that they are the worst at. When they see role models treat their teammates and opponents with respect.

It is your responsibility to create a framework for role models. This can be done in a myriad of ways, and you know best what this looks like in your particular sport and training environment.

What do we recommend?

- Create environments that make it possible to meet role models. Play with different ways to stage role models. Organise training so that young and older athletes meet each other. Make sure to give young people a mentor. Let the elite run the training at regular intervals. Invite young people to training camps, make sure they live together and cook together across grades and levels. The only limit is your imagination.

- Choose role models wisely. Choose those who represent good values. Do not just choose the tough cookies, but those who dare to show vulnerability, who dare to show that it is hard sometimes. Young people need to see that elite athletes are not perfect.

- Talk to role models about what their role is. Appreciate their role.

Literature

Henriksen, K., Hansen, J., Poole, R., & Storm, L. K. (2023). Engendering an Environment for the Optimal Development of Golfers. In The Psychology of Golf Performance Under Pressure (1. ed., pp. 68-79). Routledge. https://doi.org/10.4324/9781003299042-6

Henriksen, K., Larsen, C. H., & Christensen, M. K. (2014). Looking at success from its opposite pole: The case of a talent development golf environment in Denmark. International Journal of Sport and Exercise Psychology, 12(2), 134-149. doi: 10.1080/1612197X.2013.853473

Henriksen, K., & Stambulova, N. (2017). Creating optimal environments for talent development: A holistic ecological approach. In N. Wattie, J. Schorer, & S. Cobley (Eds.), Handbook of talent identification and development in sport. Routledge.

Ronkainen, N.J., Ryba, T. V. & Selänne, H. (2019). "She is where I'd want to be in my career": Youth athletes' role models and their implications for career and identity construction. Psychology of Sport and Exercise, 45. DOI: 10.1016/j.psychsport.2019.101562.

Ryom, K., Ravn, M., Düring, R. & Henriksen, K. (2019). Talent Development in Football-A Holistic Perspective: The Case of KRC Genk. International Sport Coaching Journal, 7(3), 360-369. DOI: 10.1123/iscj.2019-0045.

Seanor, M., Schinke, R.J., Stambulova, N., Henriksen, K., Ross, D. & Griffin, C. (2019). Catch the Feeling of Flying: Guided Walks Through a Trampoline Olympic Development Environment. Case Studies in Sport and Exercise Psychology , 3, 11-19. DOI: 10.1123/cssep.2019-0002.

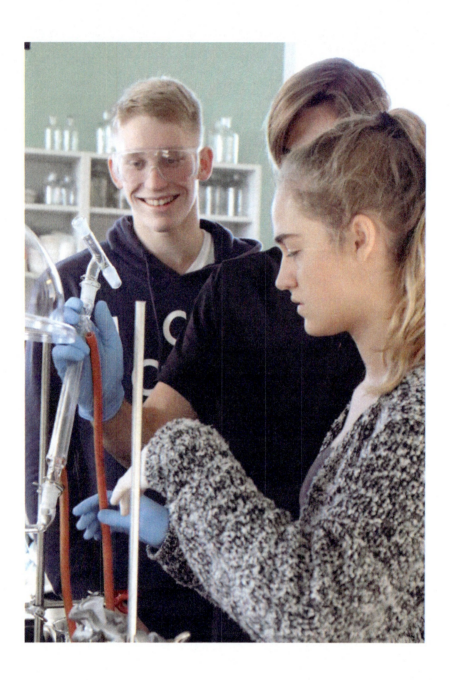

CHAPTER 13

Embrace the entire environment

We recommend that as a talent developer you do not just focus on the young people's time in training and competition, but that you look at the bigger picture. Firstly, you should look at the *whole career*. Good talent development is not just about the here and now. You need to understand where young people are coming from and where they are going. What do they need to learn from you in order to succeed in their future? Secondly, you need to look at the *whole person*. Talented young people are found in many different arenas, and their success is not only dependent on what they do in the swimming pool or on the football field. A well-connected youth life is important. Young people need flexibility from all sides.

"They need something to fall back on". This is often heard when it comes to explaining why promising sports talents need to get an education while chasing the dream of an elite sports career. Christina Teller is almost annoyed to hear this cliché. It is too banal and does not show the essence of what it means to have other important things in life than sports – even "here and now". It is more accurate to view education as something that can help support a stronger development in sport along the way, just as skills from elite sport can help increase the educational development of the elite sports student. This is one thing that is clear from her experience.

Christina Teller has more than 20 years of professional experience with young talents combining sports and education. She has previously worked at a sports school and is today responsible for Dual Career at Team Denmark.

Christina has always been curious and had a keen interest in talent development and education. She has always followed research, discussed with colleagues and visited international talent environments. "In this way, I was constantly seeking knowledge, trying it out and acquiring more knowledge," says Christina.

Dual careers are all about flexibility. Christina has seen how crucial this flexibility can be for athletes' well-being and work-life balance. And for their ability to realise their sporting potential and ambition. She has seen how athletes who are given the space to develop personally, professionally and as human beings take something with them in life. Whether they end up on top of a medal podium or not.

Although Christina emphasises personal development, she stresses that sporting development also benefits from a flexible framework and support. She mentions a whole host of current Olympic and professional athletes that she used to mentor during her time at the sports school. She is genuinely interested in their progress in elite sport.

Through thousands of individual counselling sessions, she has built up a deep insight and has a pretty clear picture of what works. "It's crucial that coaches, teachers, parents and managers look at the big picture, that they collaborate to find flexible solutions. Then the talents grow athletically, personally and academically. It really does not take much when the framework is in order," she says.

Christina emphasises that Denmark has good conditions for taking a holistic view of the talents' lives. She highlights Danish elite sports legislation, which states that Danish elite sports must be developed in a socially responsible way. "It gives us a clear value-based direction for Danish elite sport," she says. This is a prerequisite for creating a sustainable culture where talents can make conscious choices in their everyday lives. She also highlights the general Danish education culture. The youth education programmes are good at creating flexible frameworks and have many years of experience in finding good solutions in collaboration with the sport.

What are the key concepts?

The **sporting career** consists of a series of stages and transitions between stages, driven by the pursuit of an individual achievement – a peak – in one or more sporting events.

Dual career describes when a young person is engaged in their sport and an education or profession at the same time.

'The whole person' is a term used in sport psychology. It means that people are not reduced to being an athlete. Being an athlete is just one role in life among several others, such as student, employee or family member. Human first, athlete second.

Holistic development describes that development has many dimensions. While changes are happening in sport, changes are also happening in the psychological, social, educational, occupational and financial domains. Changes in one dimension inevitably lead to changes in the others.

What do we know?

Worldwide, athletes strive daily to balance secondary education with ambitious youth sports. These athletes need special flexible conditions, such as the ability to extend their education, receive additional tuition and reschedule exams that may coincide with training camps or important competitions.

Dual career is part of the problem and part of the solution

The importance of looking up, seeing the big picture and being flexible has a solid research base.

There are short-term and long-term benefits to ensuring there is more to life than sport. The most solid and unambiguous finding across many studies is that flexibility is key.

The transition from talent to elite sport often coincides with transitions to new levels of educational and professional development. Reconciling the demands of training and competition with the demands of education systems can be stressful. The challenges of combining elite sport and education have been demonstrated time and again in international sport psychology research. And they have now received political attention, for example in the European Commission's proposal to promote the development of elite sport in a socially responsible way.

The pressure of striving to succeed in two domains can put athletes at risk of burnout in sport and/or school. A study conducted in Finland found that athletes with dual career paths reported symptoms of burnout as early as the beginning of high school. Stress and burnout are the first steps towards mental health challenges as well as dropping out of sport or school. So, can't you just remove one domain from their lives to make room for the other? Can't they get an education later? Well, maybe that is a solution for some, but it is certainly not a blanket recommendation. Why is that? Because we have a lot of knowledge that shows positive aspects of having more in life than sports during the developmental years.

We know that athletes who develop in multiple arenas achieve greater well-being and are less likely to burn out 'prematurely'. Athletes with 'more legs to stand on' are better prepared for life after sport and cope better with career endings. Having a plan after sport can provide a sense of security that makes it easier to focus on the here and now. We know that the stimulation that comes from other parts of life can help maintain interest and commitment to training, especially when athletes face injuries and disappointments. And we know that dual career athletes experience better mental health and well-being.

But it requires flexibility. Without flexibility, the challenges outweigh the benefits.

The research corresponds well with what Christina has experienced in her practical work. She breaks it down for us. "Talents who are met with understanding and support to find individual flexible solutions are better protected against major downturns and fluctuations. Often it is about asking them how they are doing. Someone needs to see them and acknowledge the challenges of combining ambitious sport and school."

She continues: "Lack of flexibility, lack of support, lack of coordination or lack of understanding from coaches, teachers or parents, on the other hand, is often the direct cause of challenges and, for some, even unhappiness. But it often takes very little to turn the situation around." She cites a number of examples where someone had taken the initiative to coordinate across family, school and sport. It gave the athletes peace of mind. She happily mentions that it was actually often a coach who pointed out that the athlete was challenged and initiated a coordinated plan.

The difficult transition

The purpose of talent development is for young talents to build skills and receive support to master the transition from youth to senior. It is a critical transition that is known for a high dropout rate. Only around a third of junior athletes successfully make the transition and continue into senior sport.

In the transition from junior to senior athlete, there is a significant shift due to increased intensity of training, higher levels of competition and greater demands on the athlete to utilise their support network. It is a tough experience to go from being the best in your year to being one of many who are good and probably even better. From being the big fish in the small pond to being the small fish in the big pond. To add injury to insult, the change often coincides with difficult transitions in education, for example from primary school to high school and later from high school to higher education. At the same time, there are shifts in social relationships, where parents slowly fade into the background and are replaced by friends and coaches as the dominant key figures, and in the economic sphere, where federations and sponsors gradually take over the role of parents as financial supporters.

Research has shown that in order to manage all these complex shifts, talent needs to develop skills, build a solid support network and learn from the experiences of others. As a talent developer, you need to be aware of this.

The whole person

All sustainable sport strives to develop the whole person. This cannot be reduced to young people pursuing an education alongside their sport, although that is important. It is also important that they feel there is room for their whole identity, to be exactly who they are. This includes sexual orientation, ethnicity, gender identity, religion, career dreams and much more. Environments where people feel they have to hide key parts of who they are do not stimulate the development of whole people.

Another essential part of the effort to develop the whole person is about meaningfulness, that young people fundamentally experience their life in sport as meaningful. Research suggests that there are four key pathways to meaningfulness:

- *Connection* is about feeling part of a community.

- *Competence* is about experiencing mastery and development.

- *Autonomy* is about feeling empowered and influential on a daily basis.

- *Contribution* is about contributing to something beyond your own goals.

Sport is great for creating experiences of community and competence. But sport is not always good at empowering young people. And it can do a much better job of helping athletes feel that they are making a positive difference to others, for example by mentoring, allowing athletes who have moved to a national training centre to return home to train with their home club and inspire younger athletes, and much more. Whole people experience that their whole life is connected and meaningful.

Good environments create good balance

Finally, we will highlight some results from a study of dual career environments, i.e. environments created to support the balance between education and sport. At one point, we participated in a large project together with a number of other renowned European researchers. In seven European countries, researchers conducted case studies of well-functioning dual career environments. A key finding was – to our surprise – that the environments had an incredible amount of similarities despite being in politically different contexts, in different sports and across age groups. Here we highlight three similarities that we dare to call 'universal'. This means that they appear in different ways and in different variations, but are always present in good dual career environments.

1. In good dual career environments, there is coordination and communication across sport, education and personal life. It can be between coaches, teachers and families. It can be between clubs and federations. As a result, the talents experience coherence in their lives. We call this *integrated efforts*.

2. There are opportunities to focus on school and sport at different times. Family, coaches, teachers, friends and others understand, recognise and support the athlete's dedication to combining sport and education.

3. It is recognised that all talents need individual solutions. This requires flexibility in sport, school and family. Sport is prioritised when needed. Conversely, school is given space when it requires extra focus and attention. And this also applies to life outside of sport.

Following on from this large European study, a new one has been established that focuses on the link between dual career and mental health. The early results show a strong correlation between athletes' experience of being in a flexible and understanding dual career environment on the one hand, and good mental health and well-being on the other.

What can you do?

We believe it is important to take a broader view and help to coordinate and balance. We can learn a lot from Christina Teller's experience. When talking about what to do, Christina is quick to point out that it starts with talent developers recognising that all domains of young people's lives are important for their well-being and development. Developing young talent with a holistic approach requires an interest in young people's experiences in other aspects of life beyond sport.

Inflexible schedules can be a major barrier to sustainable talent development and can be associated with stress. Therefore, flexibility should be ensured to protect athletes from burnout. Unnecessary stress is not appropriate because many mental health issues start in stress, so for that reason alone, flexibility and a holistic approach is so important.

Flexibility can and should go several ways. We have met a number of coaches who praise flexibility when it comes to the school giving an athlete time off for a competition. But when the school asks an athlete to take time off from training to go on a school camp or study trip, it is difficult to see the value of flexibility. It has to be a two-way street. The purpose is not just flexibility in itself. A study trip is part of becoming a whole and educated person.

The is no formula for finding the right solutions. There are no one-size-fits-all solutions, even in the same environment. That is why it is crucial that talent development professionals look up, coordinate and plan together with the young athlete. It is in everyone's best interest to help them find the optimal balance between school, sport and personal life, but the responsibility should fall on a few. Who are they in your environment?

What do we recommend?

- Create a culture of long-term thinking. Support young people to have multiple legs to stand on. Few can make a living from sport, but even if everyone could, our recommendation would be that young people need a broader experience in life. Look up.

- As a talent developer, view young people first and foremost as young people and then as talents with sporting ambitions. This supports their identity development and gives them a more solid footing in life and sport. More concretely, this means that teachers should recognise and show interest in sporting goals and ambitions. And conversely, coaches should show interest in challenges and successes in school. See the big picture.

- Everyone should show flexibility in education, sport and family. Adjust training and competitions when athletes change programmes. Allow them to participate in important events like field trips and graduation celebrations. Reduce demands and expectations at school when there are major changes in sport. Not all arenas of life are equally important all the time. Flexibility in both sport and education during certain periods is necessary and should be coordinated by a qualified support person. Be flexible.

Literature

Henriksen, K., Storm, L.K., Küttel, A., Linnér, L. & Stambulova, N. (2020). A holistic ecological approach to sport and study: The case of an athlete friendly university in Denmark. Psychology of Sport and Exercise, 47. DOI: 10.1016/j.psychsport.2019.101637.

Stambulova, N. & Wylleman, P. (2019). Psychology of athletes' dual careers: A state-of-the-art critical review of the European discourse. Psychology of Sport and Exercise, 42, 74-88. DOI: 10.1016/j.psychsport.2018.11.013.

Stambulova, N., Ryba, T. & Henriksen, K. (2021). Career development and transitions of athletes: the International Society of Sport Psychology Position Stand Revisited. International Journal of Sport and Exercise Psychology, 19(4), 524-550. DOI: 10.1080/1612197X.2020.1737836.

Storm, L.K., Henriksen, K., Stambulova, N., Cartigny, E., Ryba, T., De Brandt, K., Ramis, Y. & Cecic Erpic, S. (2021). Ten essential features of European dual career development environments: A multiple case study. Psychology of Sport and Exercise, 54, [101918]. DOI: 10.1016/j.psychsport.2021.101918.

Wylleman, P., Reints, A. & De Knop, P. (2013). A developmental and holistic perspective on athletic career development. Managing high performance sport (pp. 191-214). London: Routledge.

CHAPTER 14

Promote parental partnerships

We recommend that talent developers set out to understand parents and their motivations in order to use their resources in good ways.

Recently, we came across a post on Facebook. A grown man, who we have known for many years, had posted a picture. The image was of a football match. A bunch of 14 to15-year-old boys are running around with their arms above their heads after scoring a goal. We smile. The boys look happy. The man who made the post proudly describes how his son's team has won a regional championship after a victory in the decisive match against one of the country's biggest clubs. He highlights his son's crucial role in the victory with a goal and two assists. We hesitate a little. We wonder. We ask ourselves why this man needs to share his son's achievements on Facebook. We curiously ask ourselves what kind of feedback he is looking for and look at the comments. There are many comments from family and other 'soccer parents', especially congratulations, and comments like "well done" and "important win". We think, at least the son will not see it. But when we happen to meet the man in town later that day, he is in the middle of a match report to another parent. The son stands two steps behind his father and waits patiently, like someone who has played a minor role in the match his father is enthusiastically recounting.

Maybe you recognise the experience. We are seeing it become a trend. Parents are posting their children's victories on social media like never before. It worries us. We know many coaches who feel that they are really struggling to teach young people to be process-oriented, that it is not just about winning games but about learning, development and community. But they fall on deaf ears if, for example, daddy posts on Facebook every time the team wins, but never when they lose. Players quickly learn that results are the only thing that gives recognition. This makes the coach's job more difficult.

In Denmark, youth coaches are mostly volunteers and very often parents. But everywhere, parents play a huge and crucial role in youth and talent sports. Some parents drive their children to training and games. Some parents help out during competitions. Some parents bake cakes or pack lunches. Some parents get involved in board work to support their child's club. In other words, many parents provide indispensable help. But parents can also lose sight of the fact that it is their child's sport. They interfere with the coach's decisions, criticise the club or shout from the side lines.

The vast majority of parents are keen to support their children, but they do not always know how best to do so. We have met many coaches and managers who are frustrated by parents' untimely interference. They feel that young people have become projects and that parents too often become a barrier and a time waster in their daily work.

When parents push their children too hard or interfere inappropriately, it is not only a sign that the parents are missing the mark, but also that the environment has failed in its responsibility to make parents partners.

What do we know?

Much research has been done on the role of parents in talent development and youth sport. Camilla Knight is one of the leading researchers in the field. After a career as a youth athlete in tennis, Camilla has now dedicated her academic career to researching what she calls sports parenting. She is based at Swansea University in Wales, and alongside her academic work, she is an adviser to several organisations managing youth sport in the UK.

Camilla has published many scientific articles on parenting. In these, she has explored questions such as how parents themselves experience parenting an athlete, what they struggle with, what they want and how they can best support their children. However, Camilla also found, like many researchers before her, that there is a long way from good research to behavioural change. No matter how much she researched and how many scientific papers she wrote, she still saw the same challenges in the sport. This led her to apply for funding for a dissemination project in 2017. Not a research project. She did not want to gain more knowledge. A communication project. She wanted to create a platform where clubs and parents could get help.

Camilla applied for and received EU Erasmus funding to bring together leading experts in talent development, nutrition, physical education, children's physical and psychological development and several other fields. With an eye for talent development environments, we were invited to join the project ourselves. A group of ten of us met over the course of two years in Wales, England and Norway to discuss challenges and recommendations. The result was a series of great resources on the website sportparent.eu, based on solid research but written in a way that is easy to understand. The site is highly recommended.

Below we will summarise some key points from Camilla's and others' research and from the *sports parent project*.

Being a sports parent is as difficult as it is rewarding

When understanding and working with parents' roles, the first step is to understand their experiences. What is it like to be the parent of an ambitious young athlete? What motivations drive them? What challenges do they face in their struggle to best support their children?

Being the parent of a young person who is passionate about their sport is a gift. You get to see your child struggle, grow, succeed and build strong friendships. You see them grow both as an athlete and as a person. Camilla has interviewed several parents as part of her research, and they highlight a number of key positive experiences, including seeing your child have fun, seeing your child acquire new skills, developing friendships with other parents, having a shared activity with your child, and having a joint family project.

But it is also difficult. It takes time, money and energy. It can be hard to witness periods where your child's development does not quite keep up with the others, where they struggle to make the team, or where you worry about their long-term development. It can also be difficult to know how to best support your child from the side lines during competitions. Research clearly shows that parents themselves experience competitive anxiety and stress during their children's competitions. Unlike children who are physically active, which relieves physical tension, parents have a harder time releasing tension. In other words, they observe the competition in a state of high alert, which makes it easier for them to get caught up in their emotions.

In Camilla's interviews with sports parents, they themselves highlight several challenges and difficult situations. They find it difficult to talk to their child when they are disappointed with poor results or lack of selection, to see their child get injured, to advise their child on the difficult issues of balancing school and sport, and to maintain a good dialogue with the coach when they disagree with his decisions. On a more personal level, parents highlight concerns about time and finances, and that they sometimes feel that the amount of time they spend on their child's sport can take a toll on their marriage or their other children.

There are different types of challenges

Challenges are not just challenges. One of Camilla's ambitions has been to create an overview of the types of challenges parents experience. Camilla distinguishes between three types of challenges:

1. *Competitive challenges* are about being on the side lines during competitions. It is often challenging to manage your own emotions and excitement, to see your child get frustrated or

disappointed and to talk to your child after a defeat. Competitive challenges also include keeping a good dialogue with coaches and other parents during games and helping your child become physically and mentally ready.

2. *Organisational challenges* are all about managing life as a sports parent. Talent and elite sports can be expensive, and parents are often the sole or main sponsor for the first several years. It is also often time-consuming for parents to drive their children to training and competition. The financial and time demands can affect family life and create jealousy among siblings. And then there's the issue of keeping a good ongoing dialogue with the club, national team and others involved in the children's sport.

3. *Challenges related to child development* include making choices about how much to focus on school and sports, when to specialise in one sport, and whether to attend a competition or a family birthday party. But they are also about the decisions parents need to make about longer-term development, such as whether they think their child is ready to switch clubs or try their hand abroad.

There are different types of parental support

Just as challenges are not just challenges, support is not just support. Camilla also distinguishes between four different types of parental support:

1. *Financial support* is about parents paying for membership fees, expenses for training camps and competitions, equipment and much more.

2. *Practical support* involves parents driving, making packed lunches and helping to repair equipment. When it comes to these types of support, there are big differences between sports. It is certainly easier to be the parent of a handball player going to a match in the neighbouring town than it is to be the parent of a sailor who

needs to have his dinghy prepared and transported down to a week-long event on Lake Garda, where the sailor also needs a place to stay, food etc. But all parents recognise the need for practical and financial support.

3. *Informational support* is the role of parents in helping athletes understand the sport and the many tasks surrounding it. This ranges from rules to tournament structures and, in some cases, tax regulations. It also involves helping them understand coaches' messages and decisions.

4. *Emotional support* is the key task of helping your child deal with disappointments and injuries, talking to them about their concerns, and fundamentally building a strong sense of self-worth so that they do not only feel valued when they perform on the field.

Camilla is particularly passionate when she talks about parents being role models. Children and young people learn a lot by watching their parents. Are parents only concerned with results? Do they scold when things do not work out, or do they maintain respect for the other athletes, coaches and referees? Do they only cheer for their own child, only for the best on the team or for everyone?

Being a sports parent is a journey

An athlete's sporting career is like a journey through different phases. It is often in the transitions between these phases – for example, from junior to senior – that athletes struggle the most and find life stressful. It is no different for parents. But many parents do not consider that their challenges and roles change over time.

Camilla distinguishes three main stages in the sports parent journey. When the child starts playing sports, there are no major demands. As a parent, the main tasks are to create opportunities for the child to try more sports and to focus on fun, learning and experiences rather than results.

When the child starts in a more organised programme with intensive training, the parental role changes. The child trains harder and parents are often more involved in their child's success. Parents may now be in charge of training sessions, practising technique in the garden, contacting a physiotherapist for incipient injuries and registering the child for tournaments. Overall, the amount of financial and practical support is increasing. Many parents find that they have to play a large and active role, and as they take on this role, they find that they themselves become caught up in it. Parents see their child's success as a reflection of their efforts.

When the child is selected for special talent programmes, academies, national teams or similar, the role changes again. Now the level of difficulty increases, the club or team offers more support, and parents find it harder to provide input. They are often asked to step more into the background. This can be a very difficult transition, especially as they themselves have often been gripped by their role and find it exciting to be closely involved.

There's no one right way to be a sports parent

The vast majority of parents do it well, and only a few parents are overcommitted or disengaged. The challenges differ in different sports. In some sporting environments, especially in the so-called 'lucrative' sports, coaches tell us that parents need to be *managed*. They create alliances, have opinions on team formation, make demands and are ready to move the child to another club if a good offer presents itself. Conversely, there are other environments where parents need to be *engaged*. Where you need their resources as coaches or helpers.

When parents support their children well, they can play a crucial role in developing self-esteem, motivation and happiness. Conversely, athletes also report that parents sometimes have high performance expectations and are very controlling, creating unnecessary stress and killing their children's inner drive and love for the sport.

Camilla says she is often contacted by parents with questions about right and wrong. What can I say and what can I not say? How should I behave? Can I talk to the coaches or should my child do it themselves? What can I ask after a game? She emphasises that just as there is no one way to be a good parent, there are also multiple ways to be a good sports parent. There are many bad sources of information online that are busy telling you what's right and wrong. She has also seen sports psychologists recommend that children write down rules for parental behaviour, such as where to stand, how to react, what to ask before and after a game. Camilla says that this is not a good solution either. "You shouldn't change the dynamics of a family and make children the leaders of their parents. That's not healthy." Instead, she has come up with six general suggestions for parents:

1. Children are different and have different support needs. That is why parents should talk to their children – and do so often. They should be curious and ask their children what they find difficult and what they love most about their sport. This also includes the difficult conversation about how the children perceive their parents' behaviour on the side lines or towards the team and coaches.

2. Many coaches want help, but they may also perceive parental help as interference. Therefore, parents should have ongoing conversations with coaches about how they can best support training and what they can talk to their children about. In this dialogue, coaches can also learn a lot about their athletes.

3. Parents can benefit from learning a lot about the sport, its rules and unwritten norms.

4. Parents have an important role in keeping sport in perspective. Sport is only one part of a child's life, and even though sport takes up a lot of time, it is also important that parents take an interest in school, friends and other activities.

5. Parents should always support autonomy and responsibility. They should help children, but always make sure they are doing more and more tasks on their own. Children grow with the experience of taking responsibility. Even though sports are intense and emotions run high, parents should always hold their children accountable for their behaviour. It is never the referee's or anyone else's fault, and it is never okay to hit opponents, bully others or break equipment.

6. Parents are role models and should always act with respect towards teammates, other parents, opponents and coaches.

Parent-coach collaboration is important but not easy

A strong collaboration between parents and coaches does not come naturally and is often a source of frustration. Camilla interviewed coaches and parents about the challenges of working together. She found that coaches get especially frustrated when parents do not know the rules and etiquette of the sport, demand too much of the coach's time, contact the coach in the middle of practices or during family time, or put too much pressure on the children during competition by talking about the importance of the result or posting results on social media. Coaches also find it difficult when parents undermine the coach's authority, for example, by giving instructions in the middle of a practice or game, especially when the instructions are against the coach's wishes. And when parents only support their own child and not the others on the team.

Conversely, she also talked to parents. She found that they get especially frustrated when the coach makes big differences between the children in terms of, for example, playing time and attention, has too few elements in the training that are aimed at learning and fun, and seems unprepared or organises the training poorly so that the children are left waiting too much. They also find it problematic when the coach communicates too little with parents about what is going on and why the coach is doing what he or she is doing.

This kind of frustration can only be overcome through dialogue and respect for each other's roles and competencies.

What can you do?

First and foremost, it is important to recognise that parents play a huge and important role in youth sport. They provide many forms of crucial support. At the same time, you need to understand that parents who devote so much time and energy to their child's sport are themselves deeply engaged in the whole project. They get caught up in both the sport and in helping their child succeed. That is why they are caught up when they stand on the side lines. They get excited, happy, nervous and frustrated. Their role changes along the child's journey. One moment they are expected to take part, give instructions, and maybe do some training with their child on weekends and vacations. The next, their son or daughter is at a level where they struggle to contribute and their involvement is seen as a disruption. It is *not* easy to navigate all of this. If you want to ensure parents play a good role in your sport, you first need to understand what it is like to be them.

Neither parents nor coaches are necessarily aware of all this. Which brings us back to the roles of the club, coach and federation. Parents are keen to support their children, but they do not always know how best to do so. When parents act inappropriately, it is therefore also a sign that the environment has failed in its responsibility to make parents into partners.

We recommend that federations, clubs and coaches take parents and their role seriously and help parents to support the common project in the best possible way, so that children and young people have some developing and meaningful years in sport and reach as far in their sport as their abilities and ambitions allow. This requires an ongoing dialogue.

What do we recommend?

As an employee of a sports federation, you can help local clubs to create a well-functioning collaboration with parents. You can do this, for example, by:

- Creating templates for good parent meetings

- Creating information material for parents about the sport, rules, etiquette, expectations for training volume at different age levels, etc.

As a club leader, you can invite parents to an ongoing dialogue and set clear expectations for their roles. For example, you can:

- Hold good parent meetings where you take an interest in the challenges parents face

- Develop clear values for the club

- Set clear but overarching expectations for parents, for example that they are expected to support the whole team and not just their own child. Provide suggestions on how parents can help the club on a daily basis and on special occasions

- Organise parent groups where parents can meet and share their joys and concerns and ask each other for advice. Introduce a parent mentor scheme where parents who are experienced in the sport can support parents who are new to the sport

- Support coaches in creating dialogue when coaches are struggling to manage or engage certain parents.

As a coach, you can have a good ongoing dialogue with parents and help them support the focus of the training. You can do this by, for example:

- Continuously informing them about the content and focus of the training and holding short meetings where parents can ask questions

- Making small cards with good non-performance questions for parents to ask over dinner

- Talking to parents about what they find challenging at the moment and how they experience their children's everyday life and development

- Setting times when parents are welcome to contact you

Literature

Knight, C.J. & Gould, D. (2016). The coach-parent interaction: Support or Distraction? In: Thelwell, Harwood & Greenlees (Eds.), The Psychology of Sports Coaching: Research and Practice (pp. 84-98). Abingdon, Oxon: Routledge.

Knight, C.J., Little, G.C.D., Harwood, C.G. & Goodger, K. (2016). Parental Involvement in Elite Youth Slalom Canoeing. Journal of Applied Sport Psychology, 28, 234-256. DOI: 10.1080/10413200.2015.1111273

Knight, C.J., Neely, K.C. & Holt, N.L. (2011). Parental behaviors in team sports: How do female athletes want parents to behave? Journal of Applied Sport Psychology, 23(1), 76-92. https://doi.org/10.1080/10413200.2010.525589

Wiersma, L.D. & Fifer, A.M. (2008). "The schedule has been tough but we think it's worth it": The joys, challenges, and recommendations of youth sport parents. Journal of Leisure Research, 40, 505-530.

Sportparent.eu

Part 4

Sound talent cultures

In the foundation of the book, the talent philosophy we presented in chapter 1, we championed the idea that development and well-being grow out of a sustainable talent culture. We argued that in successful cultures, there is alignment between what people say and what they do. We also argued that alignment is not enough. Cultures should be built on good, sound values and assumptions. The heart must be in the right place. We emphasised psychological safety, warmth, care and respect. We believe that sport can lead the way and show the world that it is possible to create performance environments where mental health, long-term development and medals go hand in hand.

In the fourth part, we focus on sustainable talent cultures. We will present research-based knowledge and provide concrete recommendations on how you can keep an eye on the young person's entire environment, create a group dynamic and culture where young people develop autonomy and responsibility, learn to share knowledge and, last but not least, how you can manage the culture in your environment on a daily basis.

Remember, a philosophy only comes to life when put into practice.

CHAPTER 15

Grasp group dynamics

We recommend that you as a talent developer embrace group dynamics and focus on what binds your team or training group together. Not to win competitions in the youth ranks, but because the experience of being part of a dynamic community motivates.

Group dynamics is a complex phenomenon. In the quest to understand the dynamic processes and conditions that underpin the formation, development, performance and dissolution of groups, researchers have investigated a whole range of dynamic processes in areas such as leadership, group cohesion, hierarchy, power relations, group decision-making, communication and conflict.

Talent development is about more than the individual talented young person, it is about the relationships and contexts in which the young person is part of. A focus on group dynamics is thus in line with the book's overall philosophy of putting the environment at the centre.

There are many stories of top coaches taking mediocre teams to new heights. About teams that should not (but do) beat other teams that are stronger on paper. Every so often, stories emerge that lift a bit of the veil, give a bit of insight into how it is possible, how two and two sometimes become five. We love these stories. They inspire. But often they are as impossible to understand as they are inspiring.

Flemming Pedersen knows something about this. He is technical director at FC Nordsjaelland (FCN), a football club known for its world-class talent development. He has held many roles at the club, including first team manager and talent coach, but he has always had a special love for talent development, with a particular focus on young players. We tell him about the book and ask if he wants to contribute. As always, he is open and willing to share his experiences and perspectives. This is evident when we meet with him very early in the morning the following week. It is classic that Flemming arrives early.

Flemming has set the direction for a large part of the development of FCN for many years. People at the club describe him as dedicated, honest and decent, as a man with a big heart for the young players. He is also known as a great football tactician, but it is not the tactical side of things that we talk to Flemming about when we meet him at the office. We are interested in what characterises the Superliga (the best Danish league) team, which at the time of writing has an average age of 20 years and 20 days, is the youngest team ever to play in the Superliga, the youngest team to win a match in the league, and where the majority of the players come from the club's own talent academy. It is practically a talent squad. In addition to the team being exceptionally young, there have also been some key changes. The former captain has suffered a long-term injury, and a younger captain has to step into the role. He succeeds. Together with the rest of the team, he rises to new heights. We know how difficult this role change is, especially when it comes unexpectedly. We know the dynamics. That is why we do not ask ourselves what characterises this extraordinary young man. We ask ourselves what characterises a team that can so quickly stage a new captain, give him space and provide companionship to his expectedly uncertain leadership.

Flemming has no doubts. Despite the very young average age, the team is a very strong collective. Flemming uses terms like team spirit, comradery and group dynamics to explain why the team succeeds. He knows that on paper the team is no match for the big teams in the league. And that the players are young. But it doesn't matter what they can do on paper, says Flemming. "The exciting thing is what they can do on the pitch."

What are the key concepts?

A child of many names. For years, researchers, coaches and leaders have used many terms to explain the invisible dynamics that seems to play a major role in both development and performance. Think of terms like team building, team spirit, winning culture, synergy and momentum. All invisible. All magical ingredients in the surprises of sport. All concepts used to understand the incomprehensible.

We would like to put ourselves on the line and point to four concepts that are key factors that trump all others when it comes to understanding why group dynamics is important, even though talent development is about developing the individual.

Group cohesion reflects the social and task bonds that exist between group members in a team. It is about what binds the group together. If cohesion is low, the group can easily disintegrate. If cohesion is high, the group will stay together, even in the face of adversity. Task cohesion describes when members of a group are bound together by the fact that they need each other to achieve their own or shared goals. Social cohesion describes when members of a group are bound together by liking each other and being together.

Communication comes from the Latin *communicare,* meaning to exchange messages, to do something in common, to share with someone. Communication is a dynamic process that takes place between two or more individuals. Communication is about more than what you say. It's also about the way you say something. The confidence in your voice, the warmth in your eyes and body language. We see communication in a team as an exchange of resources. Good communication gives something to teammates or the team that moves the team closer to its goal. A clear message provides direction, just as an encouraging comment can provide motivation. Poor communication takes something away from teammates and moves the team away from its goal. An unclear message creates doubt, just as a slap in the face can destroy confidence.

Roles are necessary for a team to work together. Everyone has a role. Some roles are formal and assigned, such as the captain, striker and defender, while others are informal and more social, such as the team motivator. In order to fill a role with quality, you need to know the role, accept that you have that role and see the value of the role.

Psychological safety describes the belief or trust that you will not be punished, humiliated, looked down upon or made fun of if you contribute an offbeat idea, ask a stupid question or make a mistake. Psychological safety is a prerequisite for getting everyone's ideas out there and for group members to have the courage to try new skills.

What do we know?

Group dynamics is not only relevant in team sports. Almost all talent development takes place in a group, even in what are called individual sports. It can be in a club, a national youth team or another training community.

Flemming Pedersen has no doubts. It is crucial that a group is cohesive, not only for their successful performance, but especially for their long-term development. Flemming's gut feeling is in line with the research. Groups with a high degree of cohesion are more viable than groups without. It's as simple as that.

We made a distinction above between social cohesion and task cohesion. When a group has high social cohesion but low task cohesion, the team will be a 'social team'. Members enjoy social relationships, do social activities together and take an interest in each other outside of sport. However, they are not effective at completing tasks, roles are unclear and individual members don't feel they need each other to succeed. A social team has a high level of well-being, but, strangely enough, not longevity. Something is missing. Conversely, a group with high task cohesion and low social cohesion has been described as a cold, efficient team. It is a team where members know their roles, perform them with precision, need each other, but otherwise do not want to be together for anything other than performance. There is no social glue. A cold, efficient team may win battles, but psychological well-being is not at its peak, and the team typically has a short lifespan. We see this kind of team when conflicts are tucked away and people mind their own business off the field in the final months leading up to a championship. The group may succeed, but as soon as the final whistle blows, members go their separate ways. Some sad, some angry, but almost all without the all-important pride of having won as a strong community. This kind of group does not belong in talent development, where short-term results should never overshadow long-term development.

What we are looking for, therefore, is the good team with high task cohesion and high social cohesion. A group where members recognise each other's importance, know each other's roles and can change tactics and positions during a match. Where people want to be together, do activities together outside of sport, meet and train for fun, and take an interest in each other's lives outside of sport. Such a group is efficient, has a high level of well-being and is viable in the long run.

When talking about young talents, Flemming emphasises that it is about making the club and the teams attractive. It is about creating a desire to be part of the team, to stay in the club and contribute to the community. This requires a mix of a great community and good relationships with teammates off the field on the one hand, and that the team continues to develop and perform year after year on the other.

Relational skills and communication

A football player is not just good. He is good together with someone. He is good when he knows what passes to make to each of his teammates or what passes to expect from them. Thus, in team sports, skills are primarily relational. That is why communication is so crucial. Communication is a prerequisite for targeted training, for shared values and for changing tactical dispositions during a match. This applies to communication from the coach to the athletes, from the athletes to the coach and internally between players.

In talent development, it is important that communication puts responsibility on the athletes. That a coach does not just provide answers, but asks questions. Not just telling, but also listening. Not only communicating what the young persons should do, but also what they see and feel during training and competition that should be taken into account when deciding the next step. Not only engaging with the athletes themselves, but creating spaces for the athletes to engage with each other and make decisions together.

A safe community

After Amy Edmonson put psychological safety on the agenda in business, recent years have seen a greater focus in sport on the experience of being able to speak out without fear of punishment or ridicule.

Alison Reynolds and David Lewis conducted an analysis of more than 150 teams in the business world. Their research showed that the best performing teams tended to be cognitively diverse. What does this mean? It means that these teams had different abilities, perspectives, ethnicity, gender and more. In other words, they had a high degree of diversity. But it was not quite enough. Sometimes the members got in each other's way. When they really succeeded, the cognitive diversity was combined with high psychological safety. Members could bring ideas to the table, make mistakes and ask curious questions without fear of being criticised, mocked or ridiculed. Teams that score high on both traits show curious and encouraging behaviour and creativity.

When psychological safety is in short supply, members of a group spend too much energy protecting themselves and appearing competent. It is said that they have a double task. One is their real job and the other is to make sure they do not screw up. Up to half of their energy is spent trying to control how others see them. Imagine if you could release all that energy. If they could just focus on getting the job done without worrying about mockery or harsh criticism. What were they not able to learn and achieve?

Psychological safety is important in talent development. You need dynamics where all perspectives are heard and everyone has the courage to bring their ideas to the table. This motivates in the long run, and young people need to develop the courage to contribute to solving problems and not just do what they are told. Both in elite sport and in society. The fact that this is also the path to good performance is just wonderful.

What can you do?

Good group dynamics does not just happen. Flemming Pedersen is living proof of this. He spends a lot of his energy on optimising the group dynamics at the talent academy because he knows it is a key to good performance as well as long-term spirit and well-being. He points out that when the goal is long-term talent development, you need to look beyond the individual team and ensure that the entire club or organisation is aware of the recipe for a good team. This requires a shared vision, shared values, collaboration, a clear division of roles and a strong sense of unity. At club level.

We recommend that as a talent developer, you do not just develop the individual athletes in your team or training group. Instead, you should address group dynamics and work on creating good communication, ensuring that everyone sees the value of all roles on the team and that everyone can express their opinions. It is a good idea to ask questions that do not just focus on the individual, but on the collective 'we'. What are you deciding as a team? How will you tackle this challenge? How will you bring all skills into play? How will you communicate in the face of adversity? How will you handle disagreements within the team when they arise? That sort of thing. And you should have the courage to give individual athletes feedback, not just on their technical ability, but also on how they fit into the team. What does it do to the others' courage, motivation or creativity when they communicate the way they do?

What do we recommend?

- Show interest in the way the team functions, not just the individual player. Be curious if the team is utilising everyone's resources.

- Take the lead in creating psychological safety. By never ridiculing or criticising ideas and issues yourself, and never allowing others to do so, you can create a culture where everyone dares to contribute.

- Actively work on communication between athletes. Do exercises that are all about communication. Occasionally take an athlete out of training and ask them to look curiously at the communication of others. Which communication gives team spirit and direction? Which communication creates curiosity and creativity? Which communication makes individual athletes more concerned with appearing invulnerable or saving face than actually contributing? If you have created a high level of psychological safety, you can even ask the athlete to share their observations with others.

- Help athletes develop a social and task-oriented community. Create social activities and encourage athletes to meet outside of sport. Have clear goals and clarify how they each need each other to improve.

Literature

Bruner, M., Eys, M. & Martin, L. (2020). The power of groups in youth sport. Elsevier.

Reynolds, A. & Lewis, D. (2018). The Two Traits of the Best Problem-Solving Teams. https://hbr.org/2018/04/the-two-traits-of-the-best-problem-solving-teams

Vella, S.A., Mayland, E., Schweickle, M.J., Sutcliffe, J.T., McEwan, D. & Swann, C. (2022). Psychological safety in sport: a systematic review and concept analysis, International Review of Sport and Exercise Psychology. DOI: 10.1080/1750984X.2022.2028306.

CHAPTER 16

Assist athlete autonomy

We recommend that you create a culture of autonomy and accountability in your athletes. They are not born autonomous or dependent, responsible or irresponsible. Athletes need to learn to take control of their own careers. They learn this in many contexts, at home, at school and elsewhere. But sport is a great place to develop your ability to take responsibility. At least if you create a culture where they learn it.

In recent years, Denmark has become a veritable powerhouse in cycling, and Søren Kragh Andersen is one of the many strong Danish professional cyclists. Early in his career, he was picked up by a foreign professional team, Team Sunweb. He is now with another team, but he has good memories of his time as a young professional at Sunweb: "It was incredibly positive. Of course, there were many other aspects to it than the technical aspects of cycling. I had to learn how to be a professional. As a human being, I was forced to mature quickly. Yes, and I had to learn a new language and a new culture when I moved to northern Spain for the same purpose. Overall, my experience is that it made me mentally strong."

Søren believes that his values, attitude and approach to everyday life have helped him get to where he is today. He says he never saw himself as a shining talent. "I probably had to put in even more work to achieve results. I think that definitely helped me a lot, and it still does. I have always had the courage to make choices and stand by them." Søren believes that his attitude is one of the reasons why he has a high level of skill and is therefore seen as someone who can always make a difference on the national team.

Søren seems very determined and deliberate. When we turn the conversation to what lies behind his progression from young talent to double stage winner in the Tour de France, it is clear that it is something he is already thought about. He again mentions attitude and hard work. But he also mentions something else several times: courage and the ability to make good choices. This makes us curious. How can autonomy mean so much in a world of coaches, agents and big teams with a professional setup?

Søren gives an example: "When I first turned professional, I did not choose the financially best contract to start with. I chose a team that believed in my development. I could have earned more money, but with more money comes a greater demand for rapid development. For me, the money wasn't the deciding factor, but that I had influence. I wanted to have a say in my development and that I had a team that wanted the best for me in the long term." He says that some people around him did not really understand his decision. But he stood by his choice. He seems reflective as he says: "In general, I believe that my long-term goals are by far the most important for my development. I have never chased short-term success or financial temptations. I kind of try to build it slowly, be balanced in my everyday life, stay true to myself and my values, and use that as a driver for my long-term development." I stand by that.

Our impression of this young man is that he is not only deeply serious and professional, but also self-confident and has the desire and courage to stand on his own two feet and make his own choices. We wonder where that comes from.

Søren is quick to address one part of the answer. He explains that he wasn't born with a determined mindset and the courage to stand on his own two feet. He has worked purposefully with sport psychology, and that work has been about clarifying what he wanted to stand for and how he could stand up for his values in everyday life and in difficult choices. But that started before he started working on his sports psychology skills. We will come back to that.

What are the key concepts?

There is no such thing as true **independence.** We sometimes hear coaches talk about creating independent athletes. This is a myth. No one can do it alone. Everyone relies on the help and support of coaches, teammates, family and others. We have seen a few athletes try to be the *lone wolf,* but not successfully. We believe that coaches are really thinking about autonomy.

Autonomy describes the ability and courage to stand on one's own two feet, to make one's own choices, and to think, feel and act in accordance with one's own wishes, attitudes and values relatively independently of environmental demands. Autonomy can be seen in life as in sport; in autonomous decision-making in careers as well as on the field. Autonomy is developed in many arenas, for example in sport, family, school and elsewhere.

Free initiative is a feature of good environments. It describes environments where athletes have the opportunity to take initiative, for example, to do certain exercises or organise a football match for fun or a social evening. Free initiative only lives where talent developers do not kill it, for example, by managing and controlling, by too many rules or by planning so much training that there is no room for initiative. The ability to take initiative is a prerequisite for developing autonomy.

Empowerment describes a long-term approach to empowering athletes to be autonomous, make their own choices and stand up for them. It is about giving them both the power and skills to take responsibility. In other words, it is something you do as a talent developer.

What do we know?

Autonomy must be nurtured. It needs to be fostered a little at a time in your athletes. And it starts with you. You cannot wish for autonomous athletes with one hand while you manage and control everything in detail with the other. You cannot teach them to make decisions if you make all the decisions for them. You cannot expect them to change tactics when things do not work out if they have always been guided by a strict tactical plan. Developing autonomous athletes involves a loss of control and that requires trust. Trust in the athletes and trust in the process. And it requires a well-developed feedback culture and a high level of psychological safety. No one makes autonomous choices if they are afraid of being ridiculed or punished if the choices turn out to be wrong.

Strength of character is on the agenda

Jean Côté is a professor in Canada. In Denmark, he is best known for his research on specialisation pathways, where he has shown that many hours of targeted training at an early age is not necessary for success. Together with Wade Gilbert, he has also researched the role of the coach in youth sports. Together they have developed a model they call the 4Cs. Their point is that talent development and youth sport must develop four Cs in young athletes: *Competence, Confidence, Connection* and *Character*. It is an essential point that, in addition to sporting skills or competence, athletes must develop a belief in their own abilities, a character characterised by autonomy and responsibility, and the ability to engage in communities in a positive way.

But how do you create a culture where athletes develop these traits? Jean and Wade have a number of suggestions. They emphasise that the talent developer must take the lead and show vulnerability and courage to try new things. They call this idealised influence. We would call it being a good role model. Next, the talent developer must create an attractive shared vision, not just for the athlete but for the person, set goals, not just for sporting but also for personal development, and show trust. This is what they call inspirational motivation. In addition, the talent developer must ask questions, delegate responsibility, challenge with exciting tasks and emphasise that it is a learning process. They call this intellectual stimulation. And finally, the talent developer should show interest in the athlete's whole life, their ideas and perspectives, and acknowledge their contribution to the environment. This is what they call individual consideration.

Autonomy is developed in everyday life

Overall, we know that autonomy and the ability to take control is developed in everyday life. It is not enough to tell athletes or have a famous elite athlete give a lecture on the importance of autonomy. It happens in everyday life. It has to be part of the culture.

Let us return for a moment to Søren, who talks about his time as a young cyclist. His time as a youth rider was not easy, and much of the time he was responsible for all the tasks related to his cycling: sponsors, bike maintenance, travel plans and race programmes. There was often no access to changing rooms at events, no buses for the bikes and no chef to cook for the riders. Søren was also always very curious and detail-oriented about his training. He always got involved and took co-responsibility for training plans and for the small details of his development. He wanted to understand nutrition. He did not want to be a guest in his own development. It has undoubtedly been tough at times, but it has also taught Søren to get involved, to take control. To be accountable for his choices.

Søren's story aligns well with the research on empowerment, which is a gradual process where growth in cognition, insight and self-understanding goes hand in hand with the courage to act. Athletes need to learn about themselves before they can make good choices. This requires that you, as a talent developer, are willing to enter into a real partnership with the athletes and share power. Not equally, but not all power to the coaches either.

Empowerment is not about abdicating responsibility. We know that if we ask young people, they will often just do whatever it takes to win on Sunday. It is far from certain that they have an eye for their own long-term and personal development, and it is far from certain that they have the desire to make choices and show autonomy. Many athletes thrive on clear direction from a coach who knows what they are doing. But as a talent developer, you cannot show misguided care under the guise of "I am just doing what the kids want". You must take responsibility as a professional, as an adult. The responsibility is and remains yours. You need to want something with your athletes that goes beyond winning medals, that is sustainable and does not compromise their health. You need to teach them to take control.

What can you do?

It is crucial that talent developers in many different roles are trained to carry out their work with young athletes. In our experience, it is important that adults are well equipped for the task, that they have the tools to create a psychologically safe space where athletes can experiment with making choices, stimulate athletes to tackle new and exciting tasks, restrain control and provide concrete and useful feedback. Therefore, you must first and foremost set out to support a shift in the athlete's self-perception from passive to active, set out to teach your athletes to take control. This requires you to be curious and willing to be more 'facilitator' and less 'instructor'.

What do we recommend?

- You need to lead the way by showing the courage to try new things and to talk openly about the mistakes you may make in your efforts to be curious and innovative.

- Create space for athletes to take initiative and make choices. Let go of some of the control. Give them ongoing responsibility for major parts of the workout, from warm-up to tactical drills. Give them encouraging feedback along the way.

- Work with athletes to set goals for their personal development, not just their athletic development. Make it a clear goal that they need to learn to take control in specific, defined areas and show responsibility for the community.

- Make it clear that independence is not the goal, that no one can do it alone and that they must learn to seek help and support.

Literature

Côté, J. & Gilbert, W. (2009). An Integrative Definition of Coaching Effectiveness and Expertise. International Journal of Sports Science & Coaching, 4 (3) pp. 307-323. DOI: 10.1260/174795409789623892

Olympics.com (2022) Empowered athletes bring strength to sporting organizations

Turnnidge, J. & Côté, J. (2018). Applying transformational leadership theory to coaching research in youth sport: A systematic literature review. International Journal of Sport and Exercise Psychology, 16 (3). DOI: https://doi.org/10.1080/1612197X.2016.1189948

CHAPTER 17

Encourage knowledge exchange

The key to a sustainable talent culture is for athletes and coaches to share knowledge. If you want such a culture to grow, secrecy is inappropriate. We recommend that you as a talent developer work hard to create a culture of openness and knowledge sharing between athletes, between coaches, across levels and age groups, between clubs and across sports.

At the 2020 Tokyo Olympics, sailor Anne-Marie Rindom shouted with deep and genuine joy to a journalist: "This is what I have dreamed of since I was born". The words come as she wins gold after a dramatic competition. She is one of many successful sailors to emerge from a strong Danish sailing culture. The national team is a world-class environment that has had athletes on the medal podiums at the Olympics, World Championships and European Championships for decades. Anne-Marie Rindom has also developed her talent in this environment. Danish sailing is an exemplary case when it comes to openness and knowledge sharing. The sailors share knowledge with each other, as do the coaches.

Many may also remember the Norwegian women's national handball team celebrating another medal at the same Olympics. For over 25 years, they have been at the top of the world. Several of the players who are now the mainstays of the national team were young talents in a Norwegian club environment, which we studied a number of years ago as part of a research project. Here, too, knowledge sharing, especially between players, was a conspicuous cultural feature.

Viktor Axelsen, who in 2010 received the emerging talent of the year award , is today also at the top of the world badminton elite. At the 2020 Tokyo Olympics, he secured the gold medal in a victory over China's

Chen Long, and as the whole world watched, he exclaimed several times: "I can't believe it". It is almost unbelievable when you think about it a little more. Badminton is a highly competitive sport on a global scale, with Asian countries in particular investing heavily and having far more resources than Denmark, both in terms of population and economy. So it is almost unbelievable. In any case, it requires a very special recipe to grow out of a small nation like Denmark and dominate the competition against the world's most populous country. That recipe goes far beyond optimising training, recovery and nutrition. It involves a strong culture of knowledge sharing.

These examples show world-class senior athletes performing at the top of their game right now. However, you cannot understand the success of Olympic athletes without understanding the environments they train in and come from. As researchers, we have studied the talent environments in the three sports. At the time, we did not know who would be the stars of the future. We now see that we chose to study the right environments.

In all three examples, openness and knowledge sharing was a vital cultural trait that ensured the sustainability of the environments.

What are the key concepts?

Knowledge sharing describes the processes where athletes or coaches exchange experiences and knowledge with the aim of helping each other and optimising both their own and each other's learning. It is the opposite of secrecy among coaches and athletes who see each other primarily as rivals.

Openness is an attitude that is a prerequisite for sharing knowledge. Both to share your knowledge and to accept good ideas from others.

Collaboration is the process of two or more people solving a task or working towards a goal together.

What do we know?

Since 2010, we have conducted studies of a wide range of successful talent development environments. Together with other good colleagues, we have studied the national 49er sailing team environment, a Norwegian kayaking environment, a Swedish athletics club, a football club in the top Danish league, a Danish and a Norwegian team handball club, two Norwegian football clubs, the National Elite Training Centre for badminton, a Belgian and a Dutch football academy, a Canadian trampoline environment, an American college basketball environment, a Swedish table tennis environment and many more.

There is no doubt that thriving environments share a number of common characteristics. Openness and knowledge sharing is one of the cultural traits that crosses over. They are stronger in some environments than others, but they are always present. We cannot go into detail with all the studies, but in the following we draw on stories from Anne-Marie Rindom's, the Norwegian national team players' and Viktor Axelsen's talent environments.

Knowledge sharing works

The entire research tradition of looking at the impact of environments on talent development began with an analysis of the Danish national sailing team environment and its success. In particular, the environment was characterised by talents and elite athletes sharing knowledge in a well-functioning learning environment. They collaborated with crews from other countries to optimise their training conditions to the utmost. The athletes openly shared their knowledge about gear, technique and life as an ambitious sailor. When the Danish sailors met with their international competitors, it was always something that the outside sailors looked at with deep wonder and admiration. What is it that makes you share knowledge with each other when you are also competing for the same Olympic spots? Truth be told, we were probably just as surprised as the foreign athletes, at least until we understood the DNA of the environment.

Openness and knowledge sharing were at the core of the culture of the Danish 49er national team. There was consistency between what they said, that openness and knowledge sharing was important, and what they practised every single day. In this way, the culture was consistent and became a stabilising force in the environment, providing calm and focus for learning and development. This is impressive in an environment where internal competition is inevitable. The older athletes and coaches led the way as role models.

The environment is the same today. Just as Anne-Marie Rindom learned from the sailors who came before her, today she is committed to giving back and sharing her experiences. This is one of her core values, just as it is part of the values of the sailing community. She sails a different type of boat, the ILCA 6, but the culture of the national team is the same.

After starting with environments for individual sports, the investigation continued with cases from team sports. First football and then team handball. Among other things, we investigated a Norwegian team handball club on the outskirts of Oslo, which was identified by the Norwegian Handball Federation as a very successful environment. In that club, there were also daily examples of knowledge sharing. Just in a different way, shaped, of course, by the nature of the sport. Training and matches are naturally organised around age, because that is how team sports are. But unique learning spaces were created across teams where openness and knowledge sharing was the norm. For example, there were practices across youth and senior teams to facilitate knowledge sharing on the field across levels, and communication between players in the same positions was expected. Knowledge and experiences were also shared during strength training.

Off the pitch, in the social community, there was also a high degree of openness. We saw this before training, where players and coaches gathered informally. In particular, there were discussions about school and the challenges associated with taking an education alongside handball. The coaches took the lead. They had been dual career athletes themselves and could talk about their own experiences. They shared knowledge about everything from the challenges of being an ambitious athlete to technical details.

Knowledge sharing is not always easy

So, knowledge sharing works. But getting athletes and coaches to share knowledge is not easy.

For 50 years, Badminton Denmark has managed to produce athletes capable of competing at the highest international level. Denmark has managed to maintain its ranking among the top three countries in the world and has won several World Championship medals and medals at the last six Olympic Games. That is amazing for a small country. Indeed for any country.

There are obvious challenges associated with openness and knowledge sharing when there is also fierce internal competition. In Badminton Denmark, despite fierce internal competition, the relationships within the men's elite group were characterised by a willingness to share knowledge and help each other in training regardless of position in the hierarchy. The seasoned athletes put in a lot of effort to make the next generation, the upcoming competitors, better. The observations showed that competent play was recognised by the direct opponent. However, it was also seen that internal conflicts could create a poor training environment. When there is no focus on learning and knowledge sharing, and when players are unwilling to help each other, it has consequences for the environment. It happens in even the most successful environments. In the badminton environment, it was something that was noticed and addressed immediately when the culture of knowledge sharing was threatened on rare occasions.

Openness and knowledge sharing among athletes and coaches is essential for learning. It can coexist with fierce internal competition, but can also be challenged by internal conflict. Psychological safety and recognition are some of the processes that sustain knowledge sharing. We know this not only from our case studies. It is also widely researched and recognised in mainstream organisational psychology, where a number of studies show that the reasons why employees hide their knowledge from their colleagues are a lack of psychological safety, lack of reward for knowledge sharing and internal competition.

What can you do?

Overall, there is reason to recognise, appreciate and highlight athletes and coaches who are open, share their experiences and help others. If you want to create a culture of openness and knowledge sharing, there should be no doubt that it is a valued behaviour. You do this by highlighting it in the same way you highlight when an athlete is selected for the national youth team, is a top scorer or performed better than expected in a strength test.

Knowledge sharing does not happen by itself. Especially in elite sports, where internal competition is the order of the day, knowledge sharing can be difficult. That is why it needs to be staged and stimulated. You can do this by, for example, inviting athletes and coaches to give short presentations to each other. As a talent developer, you can set up groups for coaches where they can discuss cases and situations from their own everyday lives and help each other solve them. By taking the lead as a role model. By articulating again and again why it is important. By recognising the right behaviour. The Danish Sailing Federation has given it a name: *The Danish Model.* It sends a strong message.

Knowledge sharing can be threatened by conflicts within the group and low levels of psychological safety. Therefore, as a talent developer, you need to be aware of how internal conflicts can hinder openness.

Make knowledge sharing an expected behaviour for everyone in the environment on a day-to-day basis rather than viewing it as something extraordinary. Everyone should be held accountable for being open and sharing knowledge, but this requires that you as a talent developer have created a culture where people do not have to fear being exposed. This requires openness and the freedom to share all kinds of experiences without censorship. There must also be room to express concerns. If this is not in place, knowledge sharing will become a spectacle and may have the opposite effect.

What do we recommend?

- Create a knowledge sharing strategy. Including how you will reward and recognise knowledge sharing as a meaningful behaviour among athletes and coaches. But also how you will manage the balance between internal rivalry and knowledge sharing.

- Stage knowledge sharing at all levels. Actively create situations where athletes, coaches and managers share knowledge. This can be anything from in training exercises to at the municipal level, where multiple environments in the municipality use each other in a coaching network.

- Create dialogue across the environment. Be aware of the unique learning spaces that exist in the weight room, the physiotherapy room, the club's homework café, etc. These are often places where there is a connection between athletes across ages and levels. The key people for this to succeed, both in terms of structure and culture, are management, coaches with high legitimacy and senior players.

- Reward openness. It can be easier to share knowledge if you are already outgoing. But even people for whom openness does not come naturally can benefit from learning to reach out or learning to be open. Ask athletes where they find inspiration in their environment.

Literature

Henriksen, K., Stambulova, N. & Roessler, K.K. (2010). Holistic Approach to Athletic Talent Development Environments: A Successful Sailing Milieu. Psychology of Sport and Exercise, 2010(11), 212-222. DOI: 10.1016/j.psychsport.2009.10.10.005

Storm, L.K., Christensen, M. & Ronglan, T. (2020). Successful talent development environments in female Scandinavian Handball: Constellations of communities of practice and its implications for role modeling and interactions between talents, senior players and coaches. Scandinavian Journal of Sport and Exercise Psychology, 2, 16-25. DOI: 10.7146/sjsep.v2i0.115967

Wang, S. & Noe, R.A. (2010). Knowledge sharing: A review and directions for future research, Human Resource Management Review, 20 (2), 115-131. DOI: 10.1016/j.hrmr.2009.10.001.

CHAPTER 18

Cultivate culture

We recommend that as a talent developer, you see yourself as a cultural leader. With your central position, you cannot help but influence norms and values in training groups and organisations. With an understanding of what culture is and the mechanisms that sustain culture, you can lead more competently.

In recent years, there has been a lot of talk about culture. Culture eats strategy for breakfast, said management expert Peter Drucker, emphasising the power of culture in everyday life. We have written and spoken about cultural leadership ourselves and have met a lot of interest in the subject, but when we meet Jacob Vinholt, it is the first time we meet someone with the formal title of cultural leader.

Jacob is employed as a cultural leader in a talent environment for talents from many different sports who want to do something more with their sport. The environment is also for ambitious young people who excel in music, drawing and ballet. The environment has two main tasks. Firstly, to teach participants to develop their talent in sports and culture. And secondly to contribute to a regional growth strategy in which an excellent talent development environment is a key ambition.

Jacob's most important function as a cultural leader is to create a framework for how to practise talent development in sport. It is about working systematically and with a deliberate philosophy to ensure well-being, development and performance over time. Ensuring that the philosophy becomes the foundation, becomes the culture. Jacob says: "The trick is to create a narrative that is strong and coherent enough for people to think it's cool, but also not so confident that I can't change it in two years when the world has changed. That's my job."

Jacob is also the architect of the social life in the environment. He believes that everyone has something to learn from each other, which is a healthy value. We have followed him and seen how he puts this value into practice. When he is asked for help from an athlete and he knows others have been through similar challenges, he puts them in contact with each other. He gets them talking to each other instead of giving them the answers himself. That is how he built a learning culture, he says, telling the story of athlete Anna, who was really struggling to keep track of her weekly priorities. Jacob told her to reach out to Anton because he had faced the same challenge not long ago. She did, and they both learned through the dialogue.

A few years ago, Jacob put up boards in the weight room. He wanted to have visible long-term goals and create a culture of openly sharing and being inspired by each other's goals. On the boards, each young person has their own space where they write their process goals and focus points for the week's training. Today, it works by itself and the talents write on the boards as the most natural thing to do. Jacob still shows interest in what the talents write and asks curious questions. This is how he shows that the boards are important.

Jacob seems dynamic, but is very conscious of when and how much he sets in motion. He knows it is a difficult balance. "Questioning why you do what you do creates development. It is important to do that. But people only have a certain capacity for change. Most of the time, you want to do something you feel competent and confident in. You can't change everything at once, you also need stability." He is very aware of this as a mentor to the other coaches in the community.

What are the key concepts?

Culture comes from the Latin *cultura* and can mean cultivation, care, nurturing, refinement and processing. These are elements that are created by humans. As a general concept, culture has been described as a social system of shared symbols, meanings, perspectives and social actions that are mutually negotiated by people in their relationships with others.

Culture comes in many forms. Think of team culture, club culture, international football culture and a given country's national culture. They are all interwoven. In this context, the focus on culture is understood as the culture of the organisation, i.e. the club or team, and thus as the codes and values that club members share, communicate and negotiate in social life.

A strong culture is one where there is consistency between what you say and what you do.

Culture is dynamic. People's actions are neither completely determined by the boundaries of a culture, nor are they completely free. Thus, there is an ongoing negotiation of meaning.

A **cultural leader** is someone who is *in a position to* create, maintain and, if necessary, change a given culture, i.e. the values and norms of a group. In sport, this will often be a coach or an older athlete with a high level of legitimacy. For a coach, the role as a cultural leader is one of many roles.

Cultural sensitivity is the ability to understand the culture you are in, to act in a culturally sensitive way, and a willingness to confront your own background, biases and interests in a self-reflective way.

What do we know?

In talent development research, a strong and cohesive organisational culture has been linked to the success of environments.

American organisational psychologist Edgar Schein, former professor at the Massachusetts Institute of Technology (MIT), has spent a lifetime researching organisational culture. According to Schein, the fundamental characteristic of organisational culture is that it is a product of social learning. Another characteristic is that culture is constantly created and maintained by people's interactions with each other. In this way, people's behaviour shapes culture, just as culture shapes people's behaviour.

According to Schein, all groups face two basic tasks. Firstly, they must survive and grow by adapting to constantly changing external conditions. Just think about when a sport like skateboarding becomes an Olympic sport. This becomes the starting point for developing new facilities and training environments across the world.

Secondly, the group evolves through internal integration. A new crop of talent comes in with new ideas and desires. The star of the team leaves and the hierarchy needs to be renegotiated. Social interaction changes and the culture must change with it.

Organisational culture emerges as a set of solutions, actions and values that help solve the two tasks. It becomes culture because it works.

A strong organisational culture is characterised by consistency between artifacts, values and basic assumptions. Let us return to Jacob for a moment. The environment has posters with values hanging in the weight room. These are great examples of artifacts. On one of the posters is the slogan "In it together". The poster is thus also an espoused value. It is a value that the organisation shows to the world, puts on display. But it does not stop there. Collaboration is evident in everyday life, and it is based on a basic assumption that only together can you succeed. An assumption that governs almost every aspect of the environment's life. This cohesive culture makes for a great learning environment. In cultures where values do not align with actions, there is a risk of uncertainty and confusion among coaches and athletes, which is bad for learning and development.

Talent developers can lead culture

Culture is not something that just happens. It is not something you get lucky or unlucky with. While you cannot micromanage a culture, culture is created by people and can be changed by people. Some people have a particularly strong influence. These include coaches, managers, talent developers and role models in the environment. One way to develop cultures is through leadership, or what Schein has called primary embedding mechanisms.

One such mechanism is what talent developers care about, pay attention to and check on a regular basis. The most significant mechanism that creates and sustains culture is how leaders communicate what they believe, care about and pay attention to. Imagine one club where the coach evaluates solely on results and another club where the coach is primarily interested in how the group shares knowledge and supports each other. The culture will quickly become very different.

Another mechanism is how the coach or manager responds to critical incidents. The actions taken in such situations are strong signals about leaders' priorities and goals. Is there a connection between espoused values and enacted values? The way a coach reacts when the team suffers a defeat against a lower-ranked opponent will influence the degree to which athletes focus on process and development or results and standings.

A third mechanism is the way coaches and managers allocate resources, select, promote and deselect. This is a very powerful way to communicate values and expectations. Who gets picked for this weekend's team? Is it the one who is the best right now or the one who contributes the most to the team's learning? Is there internal rivalry for spots, or does everyone have an equal right to the game as a developmental arena?

The last mechanism we will mention here is the conscious use of role models. This is a powerful mechanism for maintaining and developing culture. The strategic use of role models in day-to-day talent development can act as a clear communication of the values of the environment.

There are many good examples

In recent years, research into successful talent development environments has grown considerably. A crucial characteristic of a successful talent development environment is a cohesive organisational culture, meaning that there is alignment between what you say you do and what you actually do. This is easier said than done, but not impossible. Let us give a few examples from research.

The Danish football club AGF was successful in developing talent and was characterised by a strong family-oriented culture based on openness, loyalty and close relationships. A fundamental assumption at the club was that they were a family. One professional player who joined the club said: "It's a professional environment, but it's also [...] homely". A talented player described that once you were in the club, you were taken care of. Even in adversity. A youth player described what the family feeling meant on the pitch: "It's the AGF team spirit. It's about standing up for your teammates. If the opponent dribbles your teammate, there's always someone behind you to back you up". The fact that others have a player's back makes him more courageous. In this way, the basic assumption "we are a family" was reflected in the tactics on the pitch.

Another example is the athletics club IFK Växjo in Sweden. One of the characteristics of this club was their ability to organise daily training in large groups. This was seen as a crucial attribute for their success. The most central assumption of the culture was that good development can only be achieved through collaboration and openness. This applied to both athletes and coaches. This ingrained assumption laid the foundation for open knowledge sharing, which is otherwise difficult to achieve in the world of athletics, where talented coaches often keep their cards close to their chest and guard their secrets. At IFK Växjö, joint training and knowledge sharing was seen every day. Being part of a large group offered friendship, fun and a sense of belonging, as opposed to small competitive elite groups. In this way, the fundamental assumptions of the culture were visible in the way training was organised and in the way coaches collaborated.

In a recent study, some of our esteemed colleagues looked at a swimming coach through the lens of organisational culture. They found that the coach worked from an explicit coaching philosophy that was consistent with the norms and basic cultural assumptions of the swim club. The coach believed in training groups, flexible schedules, knowledge sharing and continuous feedback, and this is exactly what the researchers saw when observing daily life in the environment. The study showed how the coach's practices were interwoven with the club's organisational culture. It created calm, focus and a strong platform.

Back to Jacob. The talent community he leads is built around a fundamental philosophy of talent development that they work to put into practice every day. Jacob gives a few examples. Firstly, it has to be meaningful 'here and now' and everyone should take something away for life, no matter how good they become at sport. The task is to create a framework for all children and young people in the municipality to test, explore and develop their talents. These assumptions are directly reflected in the daily practice in that the environment does not select young people in and out. Instead, they provide high-quality *individualised education,* but in a *community setting across levels, interests and ages.* Secondly, the philosophy states that well-being and developing young people's social and psychological skills comes before sporting results. This is also directly visible in daily practice. They organise community dinners, book clubs and dodgeball championships, although none of these activities are directly relevant to the sport. There are several examples, but the key message is that they have a clear philosophy that they put into action. Slowly, it becomes culture, "this is how we do things around here".

To move this idea forward, we recently organised a think tank where we invited national heads of coach education and research colleagues with extensive knowledge of culture to discuss cultural leadership. We found consensus that cultural leadership is a special role and function that goes far beyond training technical and tactical skills – we call it a meta-function. It means that coaches – no matter what else they may be doing – are always creating and maintaining culture in all that they say and do.

For example, to create a positive and inclusive environment, coaches and stakeholders should be aware of the greater purpose of their training, help everyone contribute to the group, encourage cooperation rather than rivalry, support athletes to be role models for each other, and deliberately discuss norm and values with the athletes.

What can you do?

Everything you do creates culture. Especially what you do often. Whether you are late or on time. Who you pick for a game. What you ask about. Whether you act the same way when the marginal player and the star player are late. Being aware of this is important.

As a talent developer, you are a key person when it comes to creating consistency between values and actions in an environment. Schein emphasises that culture and leadership are two sides of the same coin. Culture is both what you allow and what you encourage. As a talent developer, you can manage culture through attention, rewards, role modelling and ensuring others are good role models.

As a talent developer, it is crucial that you build a high level of cultural sensitivity. This sensitivity is on two levels. First and foremost, it is about understanding how the training group is embedded in a larger organisational context. You need to understand the larger cultural layers that shape daily life. The culture of the club, the culture of the sport, the national culture. Who the young people are and where they come from. Next, you need to understand yourself. Where do you come from? What are you surrounded by? What has shaped your life values? Self-reflection is crucial.

The fundamental assumptions of the environment will, over time, influence the skills and traits of the talent. Talent will take key assumptions and make them their own. If asking for help is valued and recognised, athletes will do so until it seems like the natural thing to do.

What do we recommend?

- Take time to discuss what you as individuals and as an organisation recognise, reward and give status. What values you communicate, how you use the symbolic meaning of environmental stories, etc.

- Actively consider how you act as role models. Examine whether your behaviour reinforces a healthy and sustainable culture. Encourage athletes to be role models for each other and support them in the process.

- Critically evaluate your own understanding of what talent is. It reveals a deeper layer that has a significant impact on culture. For example, discuss who you see as talent and who you do not, and what you look for.

- Take responsibility for how newcomers are socialised and learn norms and values. Support a sense of belonging in the group, create a psychologically safe culture and help everyone find their role in the group. Encourage collaboration rather than rivalry.

Literature

Henriksen, K., Storm, L. K., & Larsen, C. H. (2017). Organizational culture and influence on developing athletes. IN C. Knight, C. Harwood, & D. Gould (Eds.), Sport psychology for young athletes. Routledge

Junggren, S.E., Elbæk, L. & Stambulova, N. (2018). Examining coaching practices and philosophy through the lens of organizational culture in a Danish high-performance swimming environment. International Journal of Sport Science and Coaching, 13(6), 1108-1119. DOI: 10.1177/1747954118796914.

Schein, E. (2010). Organizational culture and leadership (4th ed.). San Francisco, CA: John Wiley & Sons.

Schinke, R.J., McGannon, K.R., Parham, W.D. & Lane, A.M. (2012). Toward cultural praxis and cultural sensitivity: Strategies for self-reflexive sport psychology practice, Quest, 64, 34-46. DOI: 10.1080/00336297.2012.653264.

Storm, L.K. (2020). Creating a Sustainable Talent Development Culture: Context-driven Sport Psychology Practice in a Danish Talent Academy. Case Studies in Sport and Exercise Psychology , 4(1), 58-66. DOI: 10.1123/cssep.2019-0034

Storm, L.K., & Svendsen, A.M. (2021). Conceptualizing cultural leadership in physical education and youth sport: An outline for a pedagogical concept. International Journal of Sport and Exercise Psychology, 19(Suppl. 1), S437-S438. https://doi.org/10.1080/1612197X.2021.1982479

Wagstaff, C.R.D. & Burton-Wylie, S. (2018). Organizational culture in sport: A conceptual, methodological and definitional review. Sport & Exercise Psychology Review, 14(1), 32-52.

Part 5

Dynamic sport organisations

In the book's foundation, the talent philosophy, in chapter 1, we emphasised the ethical requirement that as a talent developer you have great power and influence in the lives of young people. With power comes responsibility. Only by engaging in continuous development and staying up to date can you manage this responsibility ethically. You cannot do this alone. It should be anchored in a dynamic talent organisation where everyone is curious about each other's practices, gives each other feedback and discusses values.

In the fifth and final part, we focus on the dynamic talent organisation. We will present research-based knowledge and provide concrete recommendations on how you can develop effective interactions with your colleagues and stay sharp by exploring, evaluating and developing your own organisation.

Remember, a philosophy only comes to life when it is put into practice.

CHAPTER 19

Stimulate stakeholder synergy

The talent environment does not stop at the athletes' local community. Good environments utilise all the resources available. We recommend that you as a talent developer stimulate collaboration between club, municipality, academy, federation, talent centre and other organisations that may have an impact on talent development in your environment.

Denmark succeeds in getting the best out of the relatively few athletes we have. Some of what we do well is about interaction in local talent development. The examples are many. When a school offers morning training to particularly committed athletes and ensures that it does not interfere with their school, this is only possible because of interaction. Because the clubs, school and federation agree and play together. When coaching courses are offered locally, this is only possible because the local clubs work together, often organised by the municipality and with professional input from the federation.

Ole Mathorne is one of the people who knows the most about interaction in talent development. Ole's sporting background is mainly badminton, where he has been a player, coach and member of a club board. He has tried many roles.

Ole sees himself as a practitioner. He did not really have a researcher in him, but that changed in 2016. Ole still remembers the day he spotted the question that drove him into research. Ole was involved in a conference at the University of Southern Denmark. In Denmark, municipalities play a special role in talent development, supporting local clubs with finances and professional knowledge, and this role was the focus of the conference.

Stakeholders from municipalities, federations and clubs were present in large numbers. During the discussions, it became clear that the different municipalities perceived and performed their roles very differently. Several expressed that they were not entirely sure what their role was. The associations expressed wishes that were new to the municipalities, and several club members did not even know what resources the municipalities and associations had to offer. People were engaged in the discussion, and one thing was clear. We had only just begun to address this topic.

We all went home from the conference feeling good. But Ole stayed seated. He brooded. The next day he approached us. "I want to look into this. I want to do a PhD on the role of municipalities in Danish talent development."

This was the start of a long process. Ole asked Kristoffer Henriksen to help and supervise him. Together they went to the library databases and researched what had already been written. Together they went out and discussed the idea with the municipalities, Team Denmark, the Danish Sports Confederation and others. They were challenged, did some rethinking and were challenged again. After some time, two things became clear:

1. They were on to something. There was a lot of interest. Denmark is geographically small, and it does not take much more than a few hours to get from one end of the country to the other. These are favourable conditions for interaction. Here was a position of strength.

2. It should not be about the role of the municipality alone. No one does it alone, not even the municipality. It is not the individual organisations that create the foundation for good local talent development. It is the interaction between them.

What are the key concepts?

In chapter 13, we wrote about integrated efforts. This is about coherence in the athletes' daily environments. When we talk about interaction, we move the focus a little further out. Out into the macro environment.

Several theoretical approaches and concepts have been used to describe different forms of interaction. **Partnerships**, for example, are used as a term for collaborations that are often regulated by a contract and often involve commercial interests, sponsorships and the like.

Interorganisational collaboration is used in international research to refer to concrete collaborations between organisations that allow the organisations to exchange resources such as facilities, knowledge etc. In this context, we use the term to describe the way in which talent actors work together to develop young talent. Actors will often be organisations, but can also be individuals.

What do we know?

With his research project, Ole Mathorne shone a spotlight on a new area of talent research. The overall goal was still to understand the nature of good talent development environments, but the focus was now on how federations, municipalities and clubs interacted in the quest to create the best development environments. Let us take a closer look at what Ole found and, in general, what we know.

Talent development is primarily local and multi-stakeholder

We know that the most important arena for talent development is daily training. Federations make great offers such as national team gatherings for talented athletes. These are important. But the vast majority of young talent's everyday life takes place in local environments. It is crucial to highlight the quality of these environments.

For the individual young talent who only meets the coach and teammates on a daily basis, it may seem as if the club and perhaps even the coach are working alone. But this is far from the case. There are many players behind the scenes and they all have important roles to play. The board of the club or community sets the direction and ensures that there are coaches on every team. The municipality sometimes employs a coordinator who distributes finances, acts as a sparring partner, challenges the clubs and creates forums for knowledge sharing across clubs. The federation organises national youth team gatherings that must be coordinated with local training, sets out guidelines for good training at different age levels, gathers knowledge from elite work to inspire talent development and much more. And then there is the National Olympic Committee, which influences the overall strategic guidelines for youth sports and talent development.

In other words, there are many people involved in local talent development. Everyone has a significant role to play. But it is not always a given that the different players share the same purpose, values and understanding of good talent development. As an example, we sometimes see tensions when a federation sees the sole purpose of talent development as developing senior athletes, while a club aims to win youth championships.

So it is not the individual people or the individual organisations that can explain success on their own. It is the interaction. The federation can create as many coach education programmes as it likes. If clubs do not prioritise them and coaches do not participate, they will not have an impact. The federation can create precise guidelines for good talent development. If there is no dialogue with the local clubs, the guidelines will not trickle down into the daily work. Clubs can have reasonable requests for the development of facilities. If the local government is not supportive, it is difficult to fulfil them.

Success comes as a result of good interaction between *all* those involved.

There is a recipe for good interactions

Recipe is a big word. We admit it. But good interactions have a number of commonalities that can inspire you in your daily work.

Let's go back to Ole Mathorne for a moment. He wanted to investigate good interactions. He first contacted selected federations and asked them to identify good examples. The federations each identified specific municipalities that could serve as good examples and that they thought the Danish sports community could learn from. Ole then contacted the identified municipalities. He asked them to identify one or more local clubs where the interaction worked well. Where the dialogue was good. When he subsequently compiled the list, he had 11 good examples. And then it was just a matter of getting started.

For each example, Ole interviewed the talent manager in the club, the municipality and the federation. He asked them to describe the interaction, how and how often they met, what they collaborated on, examples of specific projects, whether there were tensions and how they resolved them. Overall, he was trying to understand the nature of good interaction.

Since Ole now had quite a few interviews, the next step was to create descriptions of each interaction and then compare. What was common? What were the common features of the good interactions? Ole found six commonalities across three themes, which are listed below:

1. *Shared philosophy.* The good interactions were firstly characterised by a shared philosophy. The very foundation of the interaction was that everyone involved agreed on basic assumptions. They shared a common understanding of what talent was and what characterises good talent development. They agreed that the goal of talent development was not youth results, but long-term development. They agreed that they wanted to do something with young people beyond winning medals. Secondly, they shared a long-term vision for talent work. They did not get

caught up in discussing short-term solutions to immediate problems. They looked ahead. They knew where their collaboration would take them in five or ten years.

Sharing a common philosophy was an antidote to unresolvable conflicts, internal power struggles and short-term problem-oriented focus.

2. ***Shared decisions.*** The good interaction was further supported by good relationships, frequent contact and knowledge sharing. The relationships were described as trusting and as both personal and professional. They respected each other's knowledge, but were also happy to meet and exchange ideas. The contact itself was described as frequent and open. They met, emailed, picked up the phone and called. Everyone could ask questions, express concerns or share good ideas.

3. ***Shared actions.*** Once the participants shared a basic philosophy and had good relationships, they were able to work effectively on specific tasks. Ole found, firstly, that the meetings were concrete. They worked on solving real challenges such as designing a local coaching course, applying for funding for better facilities or supporting the dual careers of specific athletes. Secondly, Ole found that the roles and competencies of the different participants were clear and accepted. There was not a lot of energy spent on turf battles. Everyone contributed what their particular role could.

The good interaction led to joint results. Overall, the participants were able to talk about many small and large successes. These ranged from changed training methods, morning training in collaboration with the local school, a club's talent strategy, funding applications for new facilities and much more. Examples where good interaction had resulted in concrete improvements in the local talent development environments. They all emphasised that this was the goal. To improve the local environments.

What can you do?

Today, Ole works as a consultant, among other things, creating interaction in local talent development. We meet with Ole after he has been working with his research in practice for a period of time. We ask him what we can learn from his research, what we can do. Ole emphasises that the most important thing is to give interaction more focus. Set aside time for it, prioritise it, allocate resources. Making interaction work is demanding, but Ole points out that it is worth the effort. His research shows that when you make interaction in local talent development work, it has direct positive consequences for the young talents in the communities.

Ole says that first and foremost, the idea of collaboration allows us to see the opportunities and challenges of the environment with new eyes. Actors see challenges from each other's perspective, understand each other's roles and work together to solve them

Ole has seen it work, and he lets his enthusiasm run wild. "Collaboration also has the potential to address the root of the problems in local talent communities," he says, "instead of the symptoms". He has often seen a preoccupation with helping individual athletes overcome unreasonable challenges, such as the impossible logistics of inflexible school schedules and long commute times. "It was symptom management," he says. "When you gather all the organisations involved around the same table, you can address the root cause. You can create a better schedule instead of finding a slightly faster bus service".

Ole emphasises that it all starts with a shared philosophy. It is the foundation. But it is often forgotten. You meet to discuss practical issues, the desire for better showers and more lanes for morning swim. The specifics are important, but that is not where you should start. You should start by meeting and talking about what you understand by talent, what the purpose of local talent development is, where you dream of seeing the local environment in ten years. You should start by talking about what good collaboration is, what each of you can each bring to the table, what your roles are. It is not an easy conversation, and Ole emphasises that it can be an advantage to seek help to lay a good foundation.

What do we recommend?

- Prioritise interaction in local talent development. Set aside time and resources. Find the right people who represent the relevant organisations and want to commit for a longer period of time.

- Start with the philosophy. Find the common ground and direction before tackling the concrete challenges that are always looming.

- Write it down. In clubs, boards change, and coaches, elite coordinators and federation representatives move on to new jobs. Putting the shared philosophy and strategy in writing ensures you do not have to start from scratch.

- Create a clear division of roles for the interaction itself. Interactions go more smoothly when it is clear who takes the initiative, how often you meet, what you each bring to the table and what you do in case of disagreements.

- Cultivate informal relationships. They make it easier to reach out when you need a sounding board. Relationships need to be nurtured.

- Evaluate the interaction on an ongoing basis and based on a joint discussion about what characterises a good interaction.

Literature

Mathorne, O. (2021). Inter-Organizational Collaboration to Promote Local Talent Development within the Danish Sport System. PhD thesis. Department of Sports Science and Biomechanics, University of Southern Denmark.

Mathorne, O., Henriksen, K. & Stambulova, N. (2020). An "organizational triangle" to coordinate talent development: A case study in Danish swimming. Case Studies in Sport and Exercise Psychology, 4, 11-20. DOI:10.1123/cssep.2019-0017.

Mathorne, O., Stambulova, N., Book, R., Storm, L.K. & Henriksen, K. (2021). Shared Features of Successful Interorganizational Collaboration to Promote Local Talent Development Environments in Denmark. Scandinavian Journal of Sport and Exercise Psychology, 3, 2-12. DOI: 10.7146/sjsep.v3i.121379

Sotiriadou, P., Brouwers, J., De Bosscher, V. & Cuskelly, G. (2017). The role of interorganizational relationships on elite athlete development processes. Journal of Sport Management, 31, 61-79. DOI: 10.1123/jsm.2016-0101.

CHAPTER 20

Explore your environment

Imagine a club environment, a talent team, a national team, where it is an ingrained part of the culture to think and work long-term. It is an ingrained part of the culture to openly share knowledge across athletes, coaches and environments. The environment is structured around role models and mentors, with communication and coordination across athletes' life domains. There is room for free initiative and an eye for creating a broad sporting base. Special agreements have been made with schools and education, and it works well.

That is great. But how did they get there? And how can they stick to what they are good at?

In everyday life, physical trainers discuss the details of strength programmes. Coaches discuss good exercises to optimise technical details and ensure progression. The physiotherapists discuss rehabilitation and prevention strategies and try their best to implement prevention in everyday life and treat injured athletes when needed. A sports psychology consultant is attached and offers presentations a couple of times a year and individual sessions for special needs. A nutritionist has the same role in the environment.

Sounds like a good idea. Everyone is working to optimise, to find the last five per cent in their respective areas.

Everyone is motivated and dedicated to developing their own focus area. But at the same time, it is not clear who has the overall view of the environment. Is anyone working equally hard to optimise the overall environment?

We sometimes find that the quest to find the last five per cent can be at the expense of the 95 per cent, namely the quality of the foundation, the most essential. A bit like optimising the timing of post-workout protein intake without noticing that athletes in general are eating too little or too unhealthy.

What are the key concepts?

Talent development is not only influenced by the local environment such as the club, but also by larger structures such as the federation, educational institutions and municipalities. Therefore, the following two definitions are essential.

Talent development environment is defined as a dynamic system consisting of:

1. an athlete's immediate micro-environments, where sporting and personal development takes place in particular

2. the connection and coordination between these micro-environments

3. the macro environment, which is the larger context in which the micro environments are embedded

4. the organisational culture of the club or team that is the unifying factor in how to act in the environment.

Dual career development environment is defined as purposefully developed systems that aim to make it easier for athletes to pursue their ambition to combine their sports career with education or work.

A proactive approach to development describes that the members of an environment actively seek out learning and development, for example through training, evaluation, sparring or by participating in research projects.

What do we know?

Throughout our time as researchers, we have studied many different environments that support athletes at different levels and ages. The early studies were of talent environments, and some of our recent studies have a broader focus on dual career environments. They were all great environments. But they were also environments that were constantly striving to evolve and become even better. Let's look at what can be learned from them.

Continuous development of an environment requires an open and proactive approach

In chapter 13, we reported on our participation in a large European research project with researchers from Belgium, Finland, Slovenia, Spain, Sweden and the UK. Each country was represented by a research group and each country conducted a national case study of a well-functioning dual career environment.

In the good dual career environments, we really saw that the environment was continuously evaluated and that proactive work was done to optimise the environment itself. Let us give a few examples.

Belgium explored an elite sports school with a focus on the subgroup of gymnasts aged 12-18. The environment had international sporting success, low dropout rates and provided a long-term perspective for education alongside sporting ambitions. But they did not rest on their laurels. There was an ongoing focus on gathering knowledge *about* the environment in order to optimise the environment itself.

The environment itself consisted of a coordinated interaction between the elite sports school, the sports federation and a boarding school. Although it was the task of everyone – coaches, health teams, teachers, educators, parents and families – to support the gymnasts in managing their dual careers, the responsibility for coordination and integration lay with three key persons. The three key people organised ongoing professional development, evaluation of the environment and participation in scientific projects to ensure continuous optimisation of the functioning of the environment. This was done in close collaboration with a research unit that provided evaluations of various dual career services. In other words, they were constantly collecting data on how athletes perceived the environment and evaluating different concrete measures. This open and proactive approach to developing the environment is a characteristic we have seen in several international environments.

The same was true in the UK case. It was a university-based dual career environment. Also in that environment, there were systematic evaluation routines. The dual career support team received feedback from the athletes at the end of each academic year and adapted their services based on this feedback to increase their effectiveness. Based on the evaluations, they adjusted and allocated their resources. In addition, the dual career support team was encouraged to engage with the latest research to optimise their services.

In the Finnish case – a winter sports talent environment – athlete satisfaction questionnaires also helped develop the environment. The coaches engaged in sports science research. But teachers lacked development opportunities, which was a development area they had identified in their efforts to evolve the environment from a successful talent development environment to an effective dual career environment.

Overall, new trends in research show that good environments are developed through systematic evaluation and through the organisation of networks and knowledge exchange. The close interaction between environment and research was apparently crucial for monitoring and developing the environment.

Development of an environment can take many forms

In other words, we advocate for continuous monitoring and development of talent environments. It should come naturally to us. It is now common for athletes and their coaches to collect data from GPS, power meters and heart rate monitors to assess load and adapt training plans. Many environments have established routines around physical testing and physiotherapy screening. This kind of monitoring supports performance optimisation and injury prevention. However, there is not the same tradition of systematically monitoring the talent environments themselves in order to improve them.

As the examples of successful dual career environments above showed, continuous development can take many forms. We have seen environments with structured mentoring, a focus on coach education, a willingness to share knowledge, a tradition of seeking inspiration in international environments, ongoing participation in research projects and much more. In the following, we will highlight tools designed to explore, evaluate and improve the environment itself. There are a few of them.

There are tools to take the pulse of your environment

The ambition to develop credible tools that you as a talent developer can use to take the temperature of local environments is still new. But the work is well underway. Led by Russel Martindale, a group of researchers from the UK have developed a questionnaire that focuses on the talent environment and, in particular, the perception of the coach's role in the training environment. It is a reliable and proven questionnaire that can be used in talent development environments. The questionnaire focuses on five overarching themes:

1. The extent to which the development programme is specifically designed to support athletes' long-term success, including less focus on short-term success.

2. The extent to which the environment supports athletes both inside and outside the sports domain.

3. The extent to which a broad support network is available to the athlete in all areas, including experts and school teachers.

4. The extent to which the coach communicates effectively with the athlete in both formal and informal settings, for example, whether they justify their training and provide good feedback.

5. The extent to which sport development goals are coherent and aligned across the environment.

In our view, this is an important and practical tool that can help talent environments. We would like to see the evaluation of your environment also focus on questions such as whether key people talk to each other, whether athletes feel safe in training environments, whether talents feel that experienced athletes are willing to share knowledge, whether they have enough time to spend with friends outside of sport, whether school teachers and other stakeholders outside of sport support their sporting ambitions, and whether they generally find their everyday life in sport meaningful. A more holistic view.

In connection with the European research project on dual career environments, a 'monitoring tool' was also developed. The way it worked was that a series of 50 statements were rated on a scale of 1-7 in terms of strongly agree or disagree. Questions were posed to the many different players in the environment, including athletes, coaches, teachers, counsellors and managers. Key items that participants were asked to rate were whether athletes knew where to go for support, whether all stakeholders worked in a coordinated way to facilitate dual careers, whether dual career athletes were willing to support each other and act as mentors, and whether everyone in the community recognised their obligation to protect athletes' mental health and well-being.

These are just a few examples. Once all statements were answered, a score was given for how well different aspects of the environment worked. This way of taking the temperature of the environment can be a concrete starting point for identifying where improvements can be made.

What can you do?

Overall, it is important to continuously explore and develop your talent community. All talent developers should consider how best to evaluate their environments, their work and how to gain new knowledge and inspiration. We recognise that it is also a question of resources, but gaining knowledge about how it feels to be a talent in your environment is valuable. It is worth the effort.

Training and development of talent developers is also an important item on the agenda. It is a key aspect of developing environments. Everyday development and investment in the knowledge, well-being and motivation of talent developers is necessary to maintain quality in environments.

What do we recommend?

- Ensure your environment has a strategy for exploring the environment, gaining inspiration and creating development. This could be through the use of questionnaires, verbal feedback, visits to other environments or opening doors and inspiring others.

- Ensure that your environment has requirements and expectations for relevant education and a strategy for training and continuous development of talent developers. This includes coaches, managers, physical coaches, mental coaches, technical/tactical coaches, school teachers with special reference to the target group and other key individuals. You could start by discussing and applying the knowledge presented in this book.

- Create a coaching pathway for athletes in the community. In every environment, there are athletes who have a flair for coaching. It could be at the end of their active career, but it could also be that someone simply finds the coaching path more meaningful than the athlete path. Let athletes with coaching potential know that you believe they have something to contribute to the environment and create a pathway for their learning.

- Set aside resources and time for the talent developers in the community to prioritize their own development. For example, read literature, engage in apprenticeships, participate in mentoring, networking and discussion groups, or join a research project.

Literature

Li, C., Wang, C.K.J., Pyun, D.Y. & Martindale, R. (2015). Further development of the talent development environment questionnaire for sport. Journal of Sports Sciences, 33 (17), 1831-1843, DOI: 10.1080/02640414.2015.1014828.

Storm, L.K., Henriksen, K., Stambulova, N., Cartigny, E., Ryba, T.V., Brandt, K., Ramis, Y. & Cecić Erpič, S. (2021). Ten essential features of European dual career development environments: A multiple case study. Psychology of Sport and Exercise, 54. DOI: 10.1016/j.psychsport.2021.101918

Mind your mission moving forward

We do many things well in talent development. But there are also trends that worry us. It worries us when young people are pushed towards specialisation by coaches who want to advance their own careers. When youth coaches gain recognition and promotions based on results alone. It worries us when social media is flooded with posts about victories and achievements in youth sport, written by parents who are more than willing to give their children's sporting careers their all, forgetting that it is first and foremost a young person's project. We are surprised when the European football association UEFA wants to introduce national team tournaments and count points in younger and younger age groups. It worries us when national sports organisations have many good people employed to optimise performance but none to ensure the mental health of athletes.

A number of these concerns can only be addressed through sports policy. Other concerns are ones that you, as a talent developer, have a great deal of influence over. They have been the focus of this book. The recipe is twofold: a clear talent philosophy and evidence-based practice.

In this book, we have outlined a sustainable talent philosophy. We have presented solid research-based evidence on a wide range of topics: from talent identification to good environments, from mental strength to mental health and from the very close talent environment to the interaction between clubs, federations and municipalities. We have taken the plunge with a number of specific recommendations.

So far so good. But this is where the rubber meets the road.

Now is the time to put it all into action. Get out of the armchair, down that last sip of coffee. Out into the world. Out to put your new knowledge into play. See if the talent philosophy suits you. To test how the recommendations can be adapted to fit your sport, your talent environment. To discuss with your colleagues, your fellow talent developers.

From philosophy and evidence to action

"I'm not a philosopher, I'm a coach," a renowned national coach once replied when a young and unproven researcher asked about his coaching philosophy. He saw himself as a man of action, not one to sit by the window and philosophise.

We have argued that a modern, humanistic and research-based philosophy is important. It is important for you as a talent developer to be clear and consistent in your practice, for people to see your vision and want to follow you. The above-mentioned national coach is a right to a certain extent. He is not hired to philosophise. But once the philosophy is put into practice, it will make a difference.

We argued that a modern and sustainable talent philosophy is about seeing the person before the medallist, being patient and thinking long-term, putting the environment and meaningful relationships at the centre and letting a healthy talent culture be the foundation for both well-being and performance. We hope you can see how the research and evidence we have presented throughout the book supports this philosophy.

Great practice happens when a clear talent philosophy, solid evidence and you come together. Yes, you. When you are about to start working purposefully with a talent philosophy, preferably the one we presented in the first chapter, it is still important to stay true to yourself. It can help to consider who you are, what you are made of and why you are in this role in the first place. What you want to achieve and what you understand as the core task of good talent development. What values you want to stand for and what you want young people to say about your approach to them.

These questions can help you make the philosophy your own and use the research in a coherent way that suits you and your context.

When the storms rage

Sounds easy? It never is in practice.

We can guarantee that you will encounter dilemmas, doubts and resistance. You will experience management who does not know the research and just does not understand where you are going. You will experience coaches who disagree with you. You will experience parents who pressure you. You will meet young talents who stand out in some way. And then there is the fact that talent development often takes place in politically or commercially driven organisations.

When that happens, you will be faced with doubts: Should I perhaps organise more targeted training from an early age, just for these three special talents? I can see that this athlete is under pressure, but if I keep pushing for a few more months, she could win a junior medal... can't I address well-being afterwards? This young man seems totally happy playing football and doing gymnastics, but if I don't encourage him to choose now, could the race be over soon and will he even choose my sport?

There is plenty to question.

This is the time to remember the definition of mental strength we presented in chapter 6. Mental strength is the ability to take steps towards your values, even when faced with difficult thoughts and emotions. Mental toughness is continuing to act in an evidence-based way, even when you are under external pressure. Mental strength is sticking to your philosophy, even when you sometimes have doubts. Mental toughness is choosing the value path, even when you are under emotional pressure.

You are not alone

Athletes learn more and perform better in good environments. They can only fully succeed when they feel the belong and their training environment is psychologically safe.

The same goes for you. Let this be our final recommendation. Seek out other talent developers. Share knowledge. Talk to your talent community about your philosophy and how you put it into practice. Help create a psychologically safe space where you can evaluate each other, offer input and ask questions.

We promise it will help you find your role as a talent developer even more meaningful.

About the authors

Kristoffer Henriksen, MSc in Psychology, Ph.D.

Kristoffer is Denmark's first professor of sport psychology and the head of the research lab Psychology of Sport, Excellence and Health (PSYCH). He was among the pioneers worldwide to bring talent development environments to the forefront of research. He has written several books and international articles on the subject.

For 15 years, Kristoffer has served as a sports psychology consultant at Team Denmark, assisting athletes and coaches in performing under pressure. In this capacity, he has supported athletes onsite at three summer Olympic Games. Through this work, he has been involved in numerous talent and elite environments, serving as a sparring partner for various coaches and sports directors.

Carsten Hvid Larsen, MSc in Sports Science, Ph.D.

Carsten is an associate professor in PSYCH and Head of football psychology in the Danish Football Association's high-performance group. He wrote his Ph.D. on talent development in football. In recent years, he has placed significant focus on mental health in talent development and elite sports, both in Denmark and at international football academies. Carsten has authored several international articles and book chapters on talent development, football psychology, and mental health.

With substantial experience in sports psychology and talent development, especially in football, Carsten has worked as a sports psychology consultant for Team Denmark, the Danish national Football team, and the Danish Superliga club FC Nordsjaelland.

Louise Kamuk Storm, MSc in Sports Science, Ph.D.

Louise is an associate professor in PSYCH. She wrote her Ph.D. on talent development environments in handball, with a particular focus on how the culture in Denmark and Norway shaped practices. Louise has written on topics such as talent identification, early and late specialization, key figures in talent development, motivation, and many others. She coordinates a master program in High Performance and Elite Sports.

Louise has conducted several development programs in municipalities, clubs, and federations aimed at helping develop philosophies and strategies for talent development. She has organized several major Danish conferences, debates, and development days for coaches, consultants, and others working in talent development.